Praise for

I'm Not Your Friend, I'm Your Parent

"Intelligent, insightful, interesting, and indisputably fun—just what you would expect from E. D. Hill."

> —DR. MEHMET OZ
> VICE CHAIRMAN AND PROFESSOR OF
> SURGERY, COLUMBIA UNIVERSITY, AND
> AUTHOR, THE *YOU* SERIES

"There is a battle raging for the soul of your children. E. D. Hill clearly defines the fight and offers precise advice to protect kids from terrible influences. This book is a must-have."

> —BILL O'REILLY
> ANCHOR, FOX NEWS CHANNEL

"E. D. Hill never ceases to impress me. Forget the cheerleader/prom-queen looks—this woman is a no-nonsense, uncompromising, wisdom spewing, sock-it-to-ya Socrates. I secretly wish I could send my kids to E. D.'s house for a week!"

> —KATHIE LEE GIFFORD

"I picked up *I'm Not Your Friend, I'm Your Parent* with the intention of scanning it and ended up reading it in one sitting! E. D. offers a compelling mix of common sense and practical advice from someone who's been there, done that, and developed all the 'right stuff' in the process. Nothing would strengthen America more than every parent reading this book."

—JOHN ROSEMOND
AUTHOR, *PARENTING BY THE BOOK*

"Who better than E. D. Hill—a mother of eight and a successful television news anchor—to present modern day parenting issues with both objectivity and passion. *I'm Not Your Friend, I'm Your Parent* offers tangible tactics to tackle today's parenting dilemmas. Thanks, E. D., for being a parent's friend and for your guidebook chock full of tips and treasures."

—JANINE TURNER
ACTRESS AND AUTHOR,
HOLDING HER HEAD HIGH

I'm Not Your Friend, I'm Your Parent

Helping Your Children Set the Boundaries They Need . . .
and Really Want

E. D. Hill

THOMAS NELSON
Since 1798

NASHVILLE   DALLAS   MEXICO CITY   RIO DE JANEIRO   BEIJING

Published in Nashville, Tennessee, by Thomas Nelson. Thomas Nelson is a trademark of Thomas Nelson, Inc.

Page design by Mandi Cofer.

Thomas Nelson, Inc. titles may be purchased in bulk for educational, business, fund-raising, or sales promotional use. For information, please e-mail SpecialMarkets@ThomasNelson.com.

Unless otherwise noted, Scripture quotations are taken from the King James Version.

Library of Congress Cataloging-in-Publication Data

Hill, E. D. (Edith D.), 1964-
    I'm not your friend, i'm your parent : helping your children set the
boundaries they need—and really want / E.D. Hill.
        p. cm.
    Includes bibliographical references.
    ISBN 978-0-7852-2810-3 (hardcover)
    1. Parenting. 2. Child rearing. 3. Parent and child. I. Title.
HQ755.8.H55 2008
649'.64—dc2 2
                                                                    2008010176

Printed in the United States of America
08 09 10 11 12 QW 5 4 3 2 1

I dedicate this book to the biggest, most frustrating,
most unpredictable, and as it turns out,
most fulfilling projects in my life:

Jordan, Laurel, Matt, Collin, J. D., Wyatt, Sumner, and Wolf.
If you miss curfew, you're grounded for life.

Contents

Acknowledgments

Thank you to David Dunham, Debbie Wickwire, Scott Harris, Mary Hollingsworth, Paula Major, Kit Kittle, and a multitude of viewers for invaluable encouragement, information, assistance, and patience!

Introduction

No matter how calmly you try to referee, parenting will eventually produce bizarre behavior, and I'm not talking about the kids. Their behavior is always normal.

—Bill Cosby

You aren't a perfect parent and never will be. Neither will I nor anyone else. Let that statement sink in. Deal with it. Your children will never, ever be perfect from birth to death. But, unfortunately, we live in a world that strives for perfection. It's the ultimate goal. We believe we must have perfect children and, therefore, we must be perfect parents. Both are impossible!

Don't give up, though, because what is possible is, through their own successes and failures, to teach our children the rules in life, how to behave, and why it's important to keep on trying to do better so they can grow into happy, productive, loving adults. That's our job as parents. It's tedious, time-consuming, and it lasts a lifetime.

If you aren't ready to acknowledge that kids aren't perfect, including your own, then you shouldn't have children yet. When my children were young, I began telling them, "I love you more than the whole wide world, plus infinity." I still say it to them often. But I don't believe that loving them means that all I should want to do is make them happy or even that it's my job to make them happy. In fact, I remind them that the Declaration of Independence only guarantees the *pursuit* of life, liberty, and happiness. Basically, it's all there in front of you, but you have to go get it yourself. Permissive parents believe they are supposed to give their children happiness. They buy their children everything they want, let them do everything they want, then are floored when their children misbehave any way they want; so they ignore the poor behavior, since addressing it would make their children unhappy.

> *Parents are the bones on which children sharpen their teeth.*
>
> —PETER USTINOV

Confronting a problem means admitting a failure, at least temporarily. But Americans don't like to admit failure. It's considered a weakness. My best advice is, if you aren't ready for that, you aren't ready for the job of being a parent. Unfortunately, too many people take the job and either aren't prepared for it or don't really want it. So why do they have children? Some seem to think it's an obligation.

I first became aware of the pressures adult women face when I watched Princess Diana marry Prince Charles. Everyone was talking about how soon she would have a child, an heir to the throne. Within a year she had a son, and then everyone started talking about when she would have a "backup." No one talked about whether she and Charles wanted children. Society dictated she give birth to an "heir and a spare." Admittedly, the example of Princess Diana is an extreme one, but think about how often we commoners ask newlyweds when they're going to "start a family," instead of whether they want children and are prepared for the daunting job.

Of course, every woman then thinks it's expected of her, and she'll be seen as odd if she doesn't have kids. Several women I know shared with me that they were thrilled their last child was finally going off to boarding school or college because now they could "have a life" and do the things they wanted. I'm always baffled by that. It seems to me they should have determined the life they wanted before having children.

Peter De Vries said, "A suburban mother's role is to deliver children obstet-rically once, and by car forever after." Well, not forever, just for the first fifteen years after you give birth! Your family is your life. Permissive parents mistak-enly interpret that to mean children should run the family. Everything revolves around the children's ballet classes, soccer games, and cooking their own special meals each night because they don't like to eat what the rest of the family eats.

Permissive parenting will eventually drive you insane unless you really don't care how your children turn out. They will run you ragged meeting their demands. I think I actually had a bit of a break by having such a large family. Many people assume that since I have a large family, I must be mak-ing some kind of religious statement. I'm not. Oddly enough, when I was twenty, I didn't think I wanted any children. In fact, we were surprised when we found out Laurel was on the way. In a short amount of time, I positively loved a child that hadn't even yet been born. Then I couldn't think of life without her. At that point, I didn't think about the heartache and hard work that would accompany trying to be a good parent to her. Frankly, there was no one and no book that spelled out what real parenting is all about. Right after she was born I told my mother-in-law that I intended to have six chil-dren. She thought I was nuts . . . probably still does.

> *My work will be finished if I succeed in carrying conviction*
> *to the human family that every man or woman, however weak*
> *in body, is the guardian of his or her self-respect and liberty.*
>
> —MAHATMA GANDHI

While children will bring you the greatest joy God can possibly give you, they will also cause you the greatest anguish. Even if you shouldn't, you will feel that somehow you failed them if they don't turn out to be exactly the way you imagined. It's that desire to do everything so they don't fail that has become our parental albatross. It's why we're so vulnerable each time a newly minted child expert tells us we're doing it the wrong way. You cannot give a child self-respect, and you cannot build a child's self-confidence. Your job is to provide the lessons, the time, the guidance, the encouragement, and the role modeling so they can learn to create those qualities in themselves.

Thomas Edison once said, "Many of life's failures are people who did not realize how close they were to success when they gave up." So why do children and young adults give up? It's because they haven't learned how to deal with failure. The child experts told parents to focus on building their children's self-esteem. You know what happened? That concept led to a generation of young adults who are told from the time they are born that they're perfect. Every possible thing to build their self-confidence has been done for them. Yet many can't function without medication and therapy. They don't feel good about themselves, no matter how wonderful they're told they are. They act out, dope up, and think the world owes them something. Why? The experts urged us to throw away judgment. The result: instead of having self-confident kids with unlimited self-esteem, we have a record number of children taking antidepressants, and we see a staggering increase in the number of schools for "problem students." If the experts were right that unconditional acceptance was the key to happy kids, what went so wrong?

> *You should examine yourself daily. If you find faults, you should correct them. When you find none, you should try even harder.*
>
> —ISRAEL ZANGWILL

To correct a problem, you have to find the fault. You must judge whether you have done something well or poorly. But judgment somehow has become a dirty word because of the free-to-be-you-and-me, permissive-parenting crowd. The inability to judge what is right and wrong led to a justice system with thousands of depraved killers. "Hey, who are you to tell me that I can't be a murderer, and by the way, you're free to be my victim." "I'm free to drink and drive, and you're free to stay off the road." How did judgment die? We are told by the so-called "experts" that being judgmental is wrong and harmful.

Imagine this scenario: It's the sixth-grade science fair. Sally crafted an intricate spring-loaded device that will automatically close a door if the wind blows it open. She spent hours thinking about the design and putting it together. Pam decided to illustrate gravity by rolling a marble down a triangular wooden block she took from her younger sister. In today's society, both girls will get the same amount of praise from their parents and teachers. But what if Pam's parents were to say, "Sally really came up with a creative invention, and perhaps, if you had spent more time and effort, you could have come up with something more innovative"? Experts tell us that Pam might feel so badly that she'd simply quit, not even try, pull back. News flash! She's already quit and isn't trying. She doesn't have to try; she knows that good and bad are too often treated the same because the prevailing wisdom says if you judge children, they might not feel good about themselves, and that will lead to low self-esteem. Baloney! Self-esteem can't be built into children. It comes to them when they accomplish things they know are right and good.

> *Hard work spotlights the character of people: some turn up their sleeves, some turn up their noses, and some don't turn up at all.*
>
> —SAM EWING

Across America thousands of games will be played this weekend. The score will be a tie. No, I'm not a psychic. I know the teams will tie because we've been told that having a winning or a losing team will cause some people to think they aren't as good. Guess what? They aren't! You know it and they know it. Yet at the end of the game, the teams are declared tied. But wait. Does your company always tie another company's earnings statement? Does every architect who competes to design a building get to build it so that he or she feels talented? No. So how are we preparing kids to deal with the reality that sometimes they're not number one? We tell them they are *great* soccer players even when they can't even kick the ball straight. When they do finally develop the skill, we again tell them they're great. Wait a minute, they think, I'm a great player whether I do a good job or a bad job?

What is the lesson? Today there are entire schools that don't give grades because they feel grades force teachers to make judgments. Instead, they want each child to simply *learn*. They don't have to learn anything specific, mind you. In fact, I've seen some children who were given the option of skipping math altogether for a year.

The following is certainly on the fringe, but some educators have even gone so far as to say that children who think 2 + 2 = 5 are doing well. They're not wrong, you see; they're just unique and creative. They're not afraid to *think outside the box* because no matter what they say, think, or do, they will not be judged. They are perfect. Oops! Reality check: they're only perfect until the time comes to get into college or get a job. You can tell an admissions director that computing the wrong answer on tests is the way you express yourself all you want, but it won't get you into your university of choice. Yes, creativity is wonderful. But it's just as important, if not more so, to learn how to operate within established boundaries.

"The first step to getting the things you want out of life is this: decide what you want," said Ben Stein. Of course, children want everything. Left to their own devices and unsupervised decisions, they would eat candy and drink soda pop until their veins ran pure sugar. It wouldn't be healthy for them though. Why don't kids do that? Most parents won't let them. Parents make the judgment that too much candy is bad for kids. So why are parents so reluctant to make judgments about much bigger and longer-term issues? The ultimate goal is to develop adults who can make good choices for themselves and society.

The *New Haven Independent* published an article describing a seventeen-year-old girl named Sherrell Willis. She was speaking at a government hearing about a proposed curfew:

> Curfew, curfew, curfew! All we hear from you elders is curfew. Why do you think we shoot each other? To get attention. Parents, you need to understand that no matter how your life is going, you made

us, you need to spend time with us; no matter how tough your job was or how bad a day you had.[1]

Sherrell didn't mind the curfew, but she wanted to make the point that a curfew alone, a government mandated and enforced policy, wasn't going to change the real problem. Children need parents who care enough to tell them to come home, to study, to talk to them about their day, teach them, and be role models for them. Children need to be able to determine what is right and wrong, consider the consequences, and intelligently assess how to best run their lives. To be able to do that, you must do your job as a parent. Don't just be their friend; be a parent. Raise your children. Love them, but judge them carefully.

> *The world is full of women blindsided by the unceasing demands of motherhood, still flabbergasted by how a job can be terrific and torturous.*
>
> —ANNA QUINDLEN

Judging your children means you must own up to the fact that they aren't perfect. Granted, that's one of the most difficult things to force yourself to do. I can be critical about myself, critical about my husband, critical about my mother, father, and siblings. But something happens when my kids err or someone is critical of them. I instinctively want to jump to their defense. I know them. I know their hearts. Each of my children is kind, caring, and empathetic. But every so often—and sometimes pretty frequently—they mess up. When they break a small rule, it doesn't bother me much. They're human. They are punished, and life moves on. But when they break a big rule or do something I didn't even dream they might do, and so I'm unprepared for it, boy, I feel as though I've been socked in the gut. As Elizabeth Stone said, "Making the decision to have a child is momentous. It is to decide forever to have your heart go walking around outside your body."

Something happened yesterday that, frankly, is still so sensitive to me that I can't write about it yet. Of course, I hadn't made any rule about it. I never expected it would be an issue. It never even crossed my mind. I was in quite a funk all day yesterday, and it was hard work to try to think of something else. I woke up this morning, and as I lay in bed, my mind continued churning. It's so easy to give up. It would be so simple to tell myself that lots of kids have done this, it's not the end of the world, and I shouldn't address the problem so that I can keep a comfortable relationship with my child. I could ignore it. Pretend it never happened. Never tell my child I know about it. But if I do that, I've given up on both of us. This action won't ruin my child's life; no one else may ever even learn of it, but I know that it indicates there are issues that must be worked out for the child's own good. I unconditionally love my child. It's exactly that love that mandates I parent instead of pretend everything is rosy. I am a nonpermissive parent. As John Shedd pointed out, "Simply having children does not make mothers."

If your greatest desire is to be your children's best friend, if you want stress-free relationships with your children, if you find it impossible or uncomfortable to admit that your children will be disobedient, sneaky, or deceptive sometimes, don't read this book. It's not pretty. This book is the antidote to permissive parenting.

The first step is to take a large spoonful of reality. No one can be a perfect parent, but anyone can be a very good parent if willing to take the time and make the sacrifice it requires. Be strong, have faith, and if you need a little help, turn the page.

P–T–E: Please, Thank You, and Excuse Me

Bad habits are like a comfortable bed,
easy to get into but hard to get out of.

—Author Unknown

There was an uproar a few years ago in Chicago. The owner of A Taste of Heaven Café posted the following sign:

Children of all ages have to behave
and use their indoor voices.

I wouldn't think anyone needs a sign to state the obvious, but in this age of permissive parenting, they do. Offended mothers mounted a boycott! They were shocked that anyone would dare insinuate that their children didn't have every right to climb onto the counter and start waving saltshakers over their heads. Their contention? Perhaps it's a display of their individuality through creative dance and, besides, it makes little Taylor happy.

People make a big deal out of the lack of manners in children today, but have you taken a look at the behavior of many of the adults around them? A recent survey by the *Public Agenda* indicated that 79 percent of Americans feel lack of respect and courtesy is a serious national problem. An *ABC News* poll in 1999 showed 73 percent of Americans thought manners had declined in the past twenty to thirty years. And who do people blame? Parents.

Too often we expect others to do as we say and not as we do. Dinner service in a crowded restaurant is slow, and you snap at the waiter. You're running out the door when the phone rings; so you grab it and say, "What do you want? I'm busy." Do you treat friends and strangers with equal consideration? Even if your manners are generally good, everyone slips from time to time, but that, too, offers parents the chance to highlight their own mistakes in front of their children, own up to them, and say how they will change their behavior in the future. If we model good manners, our children will be quick studies although some people question whether parents are even capable of handling this responsibility anymore.

> *Teach love, generosity, good manners, and some*
> *of that will drift from the classroom to the home, and*
> *who knows, the children will be educating the parents.*
>
> —SIR ROGER MOORE

RIGHTS IN FLIGHT?

If you've flown in a plane recently, you've probably experienced the persistent nudge of little feet as the child in back of you kicks your seat. When we get on a plane with our horde, we always try to put our potential seat kickers directly behind someone in our own family. If that isn't possible, we ask the person sitting in front of our little one to please let us know if there is any seat kicking or anything else that bothers him. I don't like someone else's child kicking my seat, and I'm sure no other passenger likes it either. But I'm sure you've seen the parents who think it's their children's *right* to kick anything they want, throw food, and jump up and down. Their feeling is that, since they purchased the tickets, their kids can do whatever pleases them. Any flight attendant can tell you horror stories.

Our children haven't always been angels, but when they err, we immediately point it out and have them correct their behavior. At times we have made them apologize to the people that might have been bothered by their behavior. Because of that, there are numerous times on airplanes and in restaurants where employees will actually thank us for having such well-behaved children. I always think that highlights the plight of manners in our society. I constantly have to correct their manners, and the thought that they are better than most is pretty scary.

While punishing bad behavior is necessary, there should also be a focus on acknowledging good behavior. One waitress came to our table and in front of our children detailed the bad behavior and poor manners of children who had been at a nearby table. She then thanked our children for behaving so well. I think it really made an impact on them to hear it from someone else. They realized that good manners do matter to more people than just their parents. (And what do parents know anyway?)

Manners expert Emily Post says, "Manners are a sensitive awareness of the feelings of others. If you have that awareness, you have good manners, no matter what fork you use." That's right. Manners aren't only about which fork you use for fish. They are the rules of behavior that keep societies civil. Some people make the mistake of thinking manners are used only by a certain set of people—rich, worldly, full of self-importance. That misses the point of manners entirely. What constitutes good manners varies slightly from one era to the next, but the basic thrust remains the same—to show respect and consideration to the other human beings with whom you share the planet.

A GROWING PROBLEM

Think of throwing a birthday party. You invite the entire fifth-grade class. You want to wait to eat the cake until after the presents are opened, but one kid can't wait. And he's hungry. While everyone else is watching the present opening, he messily cuts a large section of cake and eats it. The remnants don't look too appetizing, and the other kids get angry. At the next party, someone else who doesn't want to miss out on cake decides to quickly dig in before others get to it. Pretty soon everyone is out for himself, no one is getting along, and they all are wondering what changed. Bad behavior begets more bad behavior.

> *At a dinner party one should eat wisely but*
> *not too well, and talk well but not too wisely.*
>
> —W. SOMERSET MAUGHAM

"Manners are of more importance than laws. Manners are what vex or soothe, corrupt or purify, exalt or debase, barbarize or refine us, by a constant, steady, uniform, insensible operation, like that of the air we breathe in," said Edmund Burke. And how right he is.

If you've gotten into the manners-teaching game late, you know that once children develop bad manners, it's very difficult for them to change. There's no doubt about it, it's easier not to have any manners at all. You do what you want without regard for whether you are impacting others. You say whatever you want to without any consideration for the feelings of those around you. You eat with your fingers, wipe greasy hands on your pants, and do whatever pleases you without thought to your actions and their impact on others.

According to the National Association of Elementary School Principals, the absence of manners is a growing problem. In a "Good Manners" report to parents, the Association tries to teach adults how to improve their children's social behavior, including these:

1. Stress the importance of treating others the same way you like to be treated.
2. Help your children understand the harm caused by thoughtless, unkind words and actions.

3. Role-play difficult situations to demonstrate how your child should respond. (I think this one sounds nice but would fail the reality test. I don't know a child who doesn't think role-playing with his parents is one of the worst forms of torture.)

4. Establish a list of basic good manners.

5. Teach your children how important it is to think of others, and take time to express gratitude by doing things such as writing thank-you notes.

Manners seem silly to young children and even many teenagers, which may be why permissive parents, who are desperate to keep their kids happy and carefree, don't insist that their children either learn and/or display civilized behavior. That has created a problem so big that the state government of Montana actually publishes a how-to guide instructing teens how to behave when they apply for a job. Clearly kids weren't learning manners at home, and that was impacting their job-hunting success. So the state posted "Pathways to Work for Young Adults" on the Internet to instruct young job applicants how to create a good impression. A few suggestions included were these:

1. Be courteous to the secretary.
2. Control giggling.
3. Make eye contact.

It's shocking to me that even these basics must be so infrequently used that it became necessary for a state government to address them. It's not just Montana though. I'm sure every state could benefit by following their example. Manners are not inborn. If you want your children to have manners, you must teach them manners yourself.

Children will not learn manners if their role models (that's primarily parents) don't exhibit them, or they use good manners only on special occasions. As Lillian Eichler Watson said, "Don't reserve your best behavior for special occasions. You can't have two sets of manners, two social codes—one for those you admire and want to impress, another for those whom you consider unimportant. You must be the same to all people."

Further, if you don't expect your children to display civility, they won't. One of my sons, J. D., has manners better than most businessmen, but when he pulls my chair out or opens my car door, one of our other boys teases him about "sucking up." I ignore that child and simply express my appreciation to J. D. I know the other son is watching, and while he may wish J. D. weren't "raising the bar," so to speak, at some point he will be won over by the positive comments he hears from everyone about J. D.'s politeness. My children have been taught good manners, and I expect the kids to use them.

SIMPLE CIVILITY

My dad was the consummate gentleman, and I guess it made an impact on me. I expect people to display good manners, both men and women. Growing up in Texas, I remember the looks a boy would get if he wore a baseball cap indoors. His mother would almost immediately tell him to take it off until he did it automatically.

> *Civility costs nothing and buys everything.*
>
> —MARY WORTLEY MONTAGUE

I worked as a check-out person at the Tom Thumb grocery store for a summer, and every person (except the man who was furious when I mistakenly put in the code for grapes when I was weighing his watermelon, resulting in my ringing up a twenty-five-dollar watermelon) would say thank you when I handed them their change. People would begin requests with the word *please*. Considerate, polite language and good manners were instinctive, and that really is what we should strive to display.

WOMEN'S MANNERS

Dame Edith Evans once said, "When a woman behaves like a man, why doesn't she behave like a nice man?" And that brings up the whole women's lib movement, which was before my time. I've certainly benefited from the equal opportunities that it brought; however, somewhere along the way a gentleman's display of manners became viewed as sexist, instead of a considerate human behavior. While I'm fully capable of opening a door for myself, I like a man opening the door or standing up and offering me his seat.

I recall when I was eight months pregnant with my first child and taking the subway to my graduate school class. The car was full, and not one man offered to give me his seat as the old subway car creaked and heaved from side to side as we barreled under the Charles River. At one point my belly, which was so large it was reminiscent of one of those exercise balls used in yoga classes, was prominently displayed two inches from one man's face. He still didn't budge. He was close enough to risk being hit by one of the frequent, random baby kicks. If anyone ever offered me a seat, it was usually another woman who knew what I was going through.

Even as a boy, George Washington recognized the significance of civility. Before the age of sixteen, he transcribed a document called *Rules of Civility & Decent Behavior in Company and Conversation.* While certain parts need to be left to history, such as children not speaking unless spoken to, the vast majority of the rules withstand the test of time. One of the most basic rules is that everything you do in front of someone should be done in a way that is respectful of that individual.

RESPECT IN ANY LANGUAGE

Knowing what is and is not respectful has become a bit more difficult. That does not excuse ignorance. It simply means you need to learn more and pass it on to your children. The reality of the new America is that it doesn't look the way it used to. The immigrants don't necessarily come from countries or cultures that have customs with which we are familiar. What is common to us may be inconsiderate to them. Displaying manners means you are respectful of others. One of our local school districts sent home a list of the native languages represented in the student body. There were almost one hundred different primary languages spoken in the students' homes. Since their first language isn't English, chances are that some of the basic rules of etiquette are different, too, and it helps to educate yourself and your children about them.

> *Parents are usually more careful to bestow knowledge on their children rather than virtue, the art of speaking well rather than doing well; but their manners should be of greatest concern.*
>
> —RICHARD BUCKMINSTER FULLER

My family members are huggers. We greet people with big hugs and pats on the back. However, that is offensive to some people, and good manners dictate that you try your best to not put other people in uncomfortable situations. In Muslim households, for instance, good manners and cultural sensitivity dictates that you leave your shoes outside.

The no-shoe rule holds true in traditional Japanese homes too. Mealtime is also different from American households. The "help yourself" way of doing things is highly discouraged. You wait for others to ask if you need something. You pour the drink for your companion, and vice versa, instead of pouring it for yourself.

Here's something the kids loved—and, in fact, they think it should become an American tradition—slurping. When we travel with the kids, we love basically getting lost in a town. We look for out-of-the-way places to see, stay, and eat. At a very basic noodle house in Japan, the kids were shocked when everyone around them at lunchtime began to very noisily slurp their soup. It explained a confusion I'd had since childhood when one of my mother's friends, who was Japanese, would make noise while at our house for dinner.

Since I don't speak Japanese, I wasn't able to ask people in the restaurant why they did it, but it is common.

As anyone who knows me is aware, I certainly don't advocate changing America to suit the people who come here, but at the same time, whether interacting with someone who is just like you or someone who is different from you, it is a simple courtesy to avoid behavior that will obviously offend.

INTRODUCING GOOD HABITS

I'm not sure what magical spell comes over several of our kids when they are introduced to someone. Normally chatty kids go silent. While they are usually ready to share what's on their minds at the drop of a hat, all of a sudden they have monosyllabic answers.

> *Good manners will open the doors that the best education cannot.*
> —CLARENCE THOMAS

The habit was cringingly apparent when I took one of the kids on a school interview. We were waiting in the foyer of the admissions office, and naturally, when the man walked in, I stood up to introduce myself and shake hands. I assumed my son was in lock step. Nope. His bottom was glued to the seat, and he had that slump that teens have perfected. With a smile on my face, I quickly turned toward my son and gave him the teeth-showing, clenched-jaw signal. It's the same face I've seen on the handlers at the Westminster Dog Show when their prized pooch breaks rank and begins adoringly sniffing another dog just as the judge steps up to them.

Finally, my child pulled all his limbs together as if that were a chore and stood with a limp hand extended, eyes gazing somewhere between us and the clock, which I'm sure he hoped would speed ahead quickly. What had happened to the firm hand that can guide a football thirty yards with the power of a missile? Where was the confident young man I knew? I was aghast and felt the much-sought-after admissions spot at the school slipping away.

For the next few weeks I began introducing him to everyone we saw and making him shake hands and say hello. He realized the only way I was going to stop was if he started doing it properly. He still slips, but it's better than before.

Another one of our boys, who generally is much quieter, turns into the exact opposite personality when introduced to people. When a person enters the room, he springs to action. Big smile, solid handshake, good eye contact. Good boy. Sit. Seriously, he could be onstage. He acts perfectly.

What causes the difference between the two? We'd sent both to the weekly manners and dancing class over at the community house during the school year. The fox trot proved a formidable foe, and they both gave up that fight. The manners, we thought, were the easy part. Get out of your seat, introduce yourself, and seat any girl near you before sitting down yourself. After a great deal of discussion with the boys, we think we've hit on the difference. At one of the boys' schools, there was an employee, Mr. Cosby, who would stand at the entrance each morning and greet the children with a handshake and a hello. It became routine and normal. Collin says he just does it automatically now because he's so used to it. That ability to confidently and respectfully introduce himself and greet someone will stand him in good stead as he becomes a young adult.

In this case and others, if your child forgets to do something, simply provide a quiet prompt. It isn't necessary to belittle the child. I think it is likely that forgetful children will come into line based on the positive feedback. And as Horace Mann said, "Manners easily and rapidly mature into morals." And that's the ultimate goal, isn't it?

CONFUSING COURTESIES

Some courtesies seem to be more prevalent in certain parts of the country than others. That makes teaching your child good manners even more confusing for them and you. When my boys, who attend school on the East Coast, come back from summer camp in Hunt, Texas, they display impeccable manners. It sticks with one, but another needs constant reminders. Here is what honestly happens each morning.

My son J. D. hears me making coffee and comes down to watch *ESPN SportsCenter*. As I move toward the back door, he literally leaps up and runs to open the door. He then runs ahead of me to pull open the car door. He is eleven years old! When we sit down for a meal, he pulls out and pushes in my chair. This isn't a weird kid. He's a normal, athletic, popular boy who simply has impeccable manners. It feels really good as a mother to have a son like J. D., who seems to absorb manners lessons although I do still have to remind him to take off his hat indoors. My three-year-old is already trying to follow in his brother's footsteps. He tries to open doors or hold them open.

It seems odd to me that the person I have a really difficult time with is my teenage daughter, Laurel. Her brothers attempt to open the door, and she tries to beat them to it. With five brothers she is a bit of a tomboy, but it seems that she thinks it's a sign of weakness to let someone else do something for her. When I tell her to let her brothers do it, she says she can do it herself. She misses the point.

Women can do anything for themselves these days, and graciously accepting someone's display of manners doesn't change that. To some women, having a man open the door is an insult since it might indicate he thought she was incapable of opening the door herself. What is inappropriate conduct, in my opinion, is being ungrateful when someone performs a thoughtful act. I would hope we've gotten past this. Women should be confident enough that everyone acknowledges they know how to open doors, but they could view the gesture as a common courtesy, not a confrontational questioning of their abilities.

> *To have respect for ourselves guides our morals; and*
> *to have deference for others guides our manners.*
> —LAWRENCE STERNE

One summer when I was about eleven, my parents took us to a stable that offered trail rides. Our guide was a girl of about sixteen named Holly. She introduced herself that way, and I called her that when I had a question. My dad stopped me short.

"Refer to her as Miss Holly," he said.

She protested, but my dad insisted I had to address her properly. I didn't understand it then. I'm sure she didn't either. But I get it now. By addressing a person who is doing you a service, whether you are paying that person or not, by using the proper title, be it Mr., Mrs., or Miss, you are showing that you respect the person and do not consider yourself superior or entitled. I like this quote from Lucius Annaeus Seneca: "He is ungrateful who denies that he has received a kindness which has been bestowed upon him; he is ungrateful who conceals it; he is ungrateful who makes no return for it; most ungrateful of all is he who forgets it."

SPEAKING OUT AGAINST RUDENESS

At a holiday fair at our community center one year, I happened to be overseeing the craft area. One of our children, who was about nine at the time, came over to the frame-making table with a friend and the friend's babysitter. I knew the child's parents well, and they are respected members of our town. The kids were working on the frames when, at one point, the babysitter offered guidance.

The child snapped, "Don't you tell me what to do. You're my babysitter." She then turned back to working on the frame as if nothing had happened.

I didn't know how to react. I didn't feel it was my place to reprimand the child, so I didn't say anything. I felt so sorry for the babysitter, who reacted in such a way that I realized this wasn't abnormal behavior for the child. Reflecting on it now, I probably should have said something to the child along the lines of, "It is important to speak respectfully to everyone."

Instead, I dealt with my own child. When we went home, I explained that she would not be allowed to see the girl again until I felt the girl's behavior had changed. We told her that when someone is working for you or your family in any capacity, it is incumbent upon you to make sure the person always feels respected. At no time should you convey that you, in any way, feel superior or entitled to behave in a boorish manner simply because you or your family pays him. I was surprised when she said that she had also felt uncomfortable when the friend spoke that way. She, too, didn't know exactly what to say, so she kept her mouth shut.

Over the next few years, I was able to observe the girl at a variety of functions. Sadly, her behavior didn't change and even got worse, and I think it cost her many friendships. In a way I feel partly responsible. I think that I should have said something to her mother at the time, but I tell myself it's likely that she was already aware of her daughter's behavior since this was clearly not an isolated incident. Yet by not saying anything, I was unintentionally giving tacit approval.

> *There was a time when we expected nothing of our children but obedience, as opposed to the present, when we expect everything of them but obedience.*
>
> —ANATOLE BROVARD

WHAT ABOUT TABLE MANNERS?

From A. B. in Wisconsin:

I used to live with my daughter and her family. One of my grandsons was the most unruly, undisciplined child I'd ever known, due to the fact that his parents didn't believe in the slightest form of discipline for him. He was absolutely, totally out of control, and my daughter and her husband were beside themselves as to what to do to gain any control. At restaurants he was noisy, loud, and threw food everywhere. The place looked like a garbage dump when we got up to leave.

My son-in-law left for three weeks to visit his mother, and on the way back from the airport, we stopped at a family-style restaurant. We'd been there before, and the boy had been a nightmare. As we sat waiting for our table, I leaned over and took a pinch of hair behind his left ear and gave it a quick little twist. It startled him, and tears welled up in his eyes. I immediately rubbed the spot and assured him I was not mad but said, "We're going to go in and have our meal, and you are going to behave." Sure enough, he did. My daughter was totally astounded.

For three weeks he behaved wonderfully. But once his dad returned, he reverted to his total misbehaving ways. I came in for dinner, and there was chaos as his parents tried to cajole him into eating. I finally told him to come to the kitchen with me. I knelt down, touched his hair in back of his left ear, and said very calmly, "We're going back in, and you will sit down and eat your food." He did. His parents asked me what had changed him. I told them what I had done, and although they witnessed firsthand how their son's behavior had changed, they became angry at me. In fact, they asked me to move out.

I still believe it is better for my grandson to have his hair twisted by someone who loves him than to have police, who do not love him, use Tazers and batons on him later in life.

> *Ask your child what he wants for dinner only if he's buying.*
> —FRAN LEBOWITZ

Who hasn't gone to a restaurant at some point and witnessed bad behavior on the part of both children and their parents? Usually the problem is with young children, so that's what I'll address.

Like many families where both parents work, any free time is time that we want to spend with the children. It's also nice to get a break from racing home from work and immediately starting dinner, thus, the dinner out.

Our oldest six children have terrific restaurant manners. For a time, we probably took them out to a restaurant once a week. Taking eight children out to dinner happens less often. First, people always ask, "Are those all yours?" as if part of our brains are missing. Next, a dinner tab for two adults and eight children (the four oldest boys consume the amount of food you'd expect for pro football linebackers) can resemble the operating budget for a third world country! In fact, those large bills have caused a few uncomfortable moments.

Yesterday, we had been out blueberry picking about an hour north of our home. I love bringing fresh fruit to friends, and the kids love eating blueberry pies and blueberry pancakes, so we picked right through lunch. On the way home we stopped at a deli for sandwiches, chips, and drinks. One daughter wanted a larger sandwich, but I wouldn't let her get it because she's been trying to lose a bit of weight before tryouts for her high school field hockey team. She looked at the deli man—the deli man who clearly had never worried about trying out for a sports team—who gave a sympathizing look back and said, "Well, Mom's paying so that's what goes."

After making all the sandwiches and the kids had opened the chip bags and drinks, he handed me the tab. Guess what? Right, I didn't have enough money. In fact, I didn't have any money. As the wide-eyed, gaping mouth, "Oh my gosh! What am I going to do?" look crossed my face, my daughter rolled her eyes and said, "I've got money." I think to try and make light of the situation, the deli man said, "Good thing for allowances."

Oops, wrong comment. She shot one of those looks at me that I'm sure you would recognize and then responded to him, "I don't get an allowance. I work full-time . . . in a deli."

Ouch.

For the most part we've stopped going out to restaurants, except for special occasions. The problem is the two youngest. They start singing. They use their knives and forks to recreate the sound of an off-key bell choir performing a tune but whose members can't read music. They surreptitiously attempt to drop every green item from their plates onto the floor. They *always* manage to knock over at least one glass while reaching across the table for something. And I swear their arms have radar, honing in on the glass that contains the cranberry juice instead of the water. It got so bad that even the big kids were embarrassed! What had happened? Our older children had behaved so well at restaurants when they were little that it was quite common for managers and other patrons to stop by the table to comment on it. I think it's our fault.

With the first kids we diligently reminded them what the expectations were when we went out to eat. We would go through the proper manners and remind them about indoor voices. The moment they stepped out of line, we would explain the ramifications of their behavior on the other people in the restaurant. We'd explain that they had gone out so they would have time to spend together and talk without needing to focus on cooking, clearing tables, and doing dishes. They wanted an escape. We'd explain how hard the waiters work to clean up tables to get ready for the next customers and that by dropping food and spilling drinks they were making someone's job more difficult. They got it, and we would continue with our adult conversation.

So what happened to the two youngest? We changed our procedure. Before, it was also in our best interest to handle the problem right away because it impeded our ability to have a discussion. But with a lot of children around, there are always numerous conversations going on, and instead of speaking with each other, we are usually talking to one of the kids. If we didn't have time to notice what the little ones were doing, we just thought the older kids would handle the problem. Instead, no one did, so the youngest amused themselves and the next two older ones, who also seemed to egg on their antics. We weren't focused on doing *our* job. Now, on the infrequent occasion that we go out, we make sure the youngest sit near us, and we focus on helping them learn proper behavior.

IT'S NOW OR LATER

Fred Astaire said, "The hardest job kids face today is learning good manners without seeing any." And in truth, busy parents can be the worst role models, and later they wonder why their children don't behave better. Some of the old etiquette rules are so outdated though that it is tempting to dismiss them *all* when we're in a rush. And it seems most modern meals are a rush.

My folks were generally rules sticklers, but they forgot one thing, and it turned into a very embarrassing situation for me when I was twenty. I was invited to attend a business dinner with my date's client. We went to a very nice, expense-account type restaurant. I knew which fork to use and even dealt with finger bowls with ease. Then the bread arrived.

Now, down in Texas one of my favorite restaurants was run by an old man named Jasper. He'd wake up in the morning and decide how much barbecue he felt like selling, and that's how much he'd cook. The restaurant was in a rundown former service station. Jasper would open the garage doors, and you'd walk in. He had some long, cafeteria-style old wooden tables and rickety chairs. There was no restroom, but there was a sink where I think the mechanics used to wash up, and he had soap and a roll of paper towels there for people who preferred to clean their hands that way instead of simply sucking the barbecue sauce off their fingers.

Jasper had a production line going. He only cooked one type of barbecue, and he only served it one way. He'd take a piece of wax paper, put some barbecue on it, garnish it with a couple of pickle slices, and slap a roll on top. He figured we'd fix it up just the way we liked it. I loved splitting the roll right down the middle, adding a bit of butter, and then the brisket and pickles. My first bite was always a big one.

Anyway, back to the fancy-pants restaurant. A roll was put on my bread plate. It was steaming, clearly just out of the oven. A dish of butter was in front of me. I did what I always did at home and had done at other restaurants—I split it, spread the butter, and took a big bite. The look on my date's face indicated I'd just committed the faux pas of the century.

In front of everybody he said, "Don't you break your roll?" and he delicately broke off a piece and added a small dab of butter to it.

When I got home, I called my mother and explained what had happened. She seemed surprised. "Of course, you are supposed to break off a small bite instead of taking a big bite out of the roll," she said.

Well, how was I supposed to know? This was one lesson they skipped. I guess they just figured I'd pick up on their way of doing it, but they never explained that was the correct way.

Frankly, this date was a bit of a jerk. At the most he should have discreetly whispered to me that I should break the bread, instead of announcing it so loudly that the hostess at the restaurant across the street could hear him.

The lesson is if you don't take the time to properly teach your children good table manners, it will be difficult for them later in life. If you aren't sure exactly what to teach your children, go to the library. There are numerous good table manners books. In addition, there are people who run etiquette classes.

HERE ARE THE BASIC LESSONS AT OUR HOUSE

By age two we expect the children to say *please* and *thank you* each time they request something at the table. Bear in mind that those words frequently come out as *peas* and *fank u*, but by and by they'll get the drill. The idea is to start early and make good manners rote.

By age three they are expected to put their napkins in their laps. Often they forget until a sibling reminds them. Older brothers and sisters always seem quick to point out something they've done that another child has forgotten! At dinner last week, Wyatt whipped his napkin into his lap and announced it before the other children had even gotten seated. There were a couple of sets of rolled eyes, but the other kids put their napkins in their laps too. Early on we went through a period where the kids were forgetting to put their napkins in their laps almost every meal. We made the rule that the last person to get his napkin into his lap has to clear the table. I can't tell you how quickly the issue was put to rest. Let's just say that the napkin placing at mealtime was done in such a flash that a matador in Spain would have been impressed.

The benefit for little ones who have older siblings is that while children listen to parents and learn from them, they are really eager to act more like their older siblings (whom they usually idolize) so they can be "big boys and girls."

By age four they are almost completely cured of playing with food, although blowing milk bubbles still holds a perverse fascination. They should also be able to clear their places and get their plates to the sink without dropping them too many days out of the week. If it's a half-eaten bowl of soup, I sometimes ask the bigger kids to help out.

By age five they should know not to speak with food in their mouths and to chew with their lips closed. In addition, they should be able to keep in check their temptation to grab their favorite food, like a cookie, from someone else's plate.

By age six, at the latest, they should remember to ask to be excused from the table and to have food items passed to them, instead of reaching in front of someone else to get them.

SAYING GRACE

Here's one of the toughest rules in our family: children must wait until everyone is seated and thanks given before starting to eat. We have a busy household, probably a lot like yours. The little kids want to eat earlier, and the older kids don't get home from afternoon sports practice until later. My husband sometimes makes it, but other times he gets stuck in traffic. If it's apparent that food will get cold if children have to wait, then we have them say grace and begin.

> *The value of consistent prayer is not that*
> *He will hear us, but that we will hear Him.*
> —WILLIAM MCGILL

Grace, ah, at first, that is sometimes a challenge. Here's what we do: if a child begins to giggle during grace, at the next meal he gets to say grace while everyone else listens. If the child uses it as a time to thank God for odd things, we figure the more things he's grateful for, the better, and we let it go. But if the monologue brings on howls from the rest of the table, the child must continue to lead grace at each meal until he does it properly. It gets tough on a kid to think up funny things to say to try to get his siblings to laugh, so he settles down pretty quickly and gets on with it.

YES, MA'AM!

People now often marry someone who may have been raised in a completely different part of the country. While we are all Americans, sections of America are like different countries, each with its own particular customs and norms. A common courtesy, at least where I'm from, seems to be gaining in controversy elsewhere in the country, particularly the North and upper Midwest. Even *Dear Abby* has been roped into the fray:

Dear Abby:
  I may be alone in my thoughts on this subject, but I feel that addressing a woman as *ma'am* is an extremely derogatory term. I believe it is a derivative of *mammy* and simply a way of keeping a woman in her place.
  How would any man like to be called *geezer* or *old goat* on a regular basis? I regard ma'am in the same negative light.
  How can I politely, yet firmly, respond to those who persist in their rude behavior when I am called ma'am?
                                    Definitely Not Your Ma'am in South Carolina

Dear Definitely Not:
  You must be a recent transplant to the South because south of the Mason-Dixon (and also in the military), to address a woman as ma'am shows respect. I don't know where you got the idea that ma'am is a derivative of mammy, but it's a huge mistake, and I hope you haven't said it to anyone else.
  Ma'am is a contraction of the word *madam*, a form of respectful address to an adult—usually married—woman. If you prefer to be

called something else, ask the person to call you Lisa, Ms. Jones, etc. But please don't pick a fight, or you will look foolish.

Abby[1]

"Definitely Not" isn't alone. My sister has a friend who has also run into trouble with this. She is from South Carolina and has two wonderfully behaved teenage boys, who were raised in South Carolina until preteen years and then moved north. My sister says she will never forget her first meeting with these boys. They got her attention with, "Excuse me, ma'am." She was so impressed to hear this coming from a child without parental prompting that she called their mother to let her know how well mannered her children were and what a favorable impression they had made. Parents need to get the good phone calls about their children, too, especially this lady, who then relayed a recent experience.

Her youngest boy had just been *reprimanded* by the principal of his school for saying "Yes, ma'am" in answer to a question. The principal was so offended that she called the mother about this "show of disrespect." Imagine an educator punishing a child for being respectful!

My sister's phone call couldn't have come at a better time for this parent, offering her support for teaching her children to display courtesy and respect when speaking with someone—the right thing.

Being raised in Texas, I was brought up to address others as ma'am or sir as a show of respect and common courtesy. As a young girl, I can still picture my father getting the attention of a store clerk with a simple, "Excuse me, ma'am." I talk about role modeling for your children, and this is a good example. I saw my father speak respectfully to a store clerk, and his behavior stuck with me. I teach my children that this simple courtesy goes a long way.

Frankly, it's harder to explain to some adults why this is so important. My youngest two attend preschool. Each day I have them shake hands with the principal at the front door, look her in the eye, and say "Good morning, ma'am." Ditto when they walk into their classrooms. The principal is always supportive of this and congratulates them when they give her a solid handshake and maintain eye contact. However, a number of teachers have said, "Oh, just have them call me by my first name." They believe it makes the children feel closer and more comfortable with them. That may be absolutely true, but in just a few years when they're in second grade, if they walk into the room and say, "Hey there, Judy" to their teacher, it's not going to be treated the same way.

Further, teachers deserve to get more respect. Why are we shocked at the lack of respect shown teachers in many junior high and high schools? Saying ma'am or sir may seem trivial, but it's those little things that create an atmosphere of civility. Teachers are the superiors. They are older, wiser, and charged with educating our children. Kids should view them as the authority figure and treat them that way. In the long term, this show of respect for others, both young and old, will pay off with friends, jobs, and more.

Even in the martial art sport of Taekwondo, this courtesy is shown in its oath: "Sir, I will practice in the Spirit of Taekwondo, with Courtesy for fellow students, Loyalty for my instructor, and Respect for my juniors and seniors, sir."

PHONE MANNERS

Bill DeWitt noted: "The bathtub was invented in 1850 and the telephone in 1875. In other words, if you had been living in 1850, you could have sat in the bathtub for twenty-five years without having to answer the phone." What luxury!

"One ringy-dingy . . . Two ringy-dingy." Lily Tomlin's character, Ernestine, the telephone operator, is a classic. Her comedy on the variety program *Rowan and Martin's Laugh-In* made the phrase an instant hit. Ernestine was the proper-looking operator who frustrated every well-meaning telephone customer. She would recite "one ringy-dingy [pause], two ringy-dingy [pause], three ringy-dingy [pause]" while intermittently snorting like a pig as she waited for the phone call to connect to another customer. When someone finally answered, she would continue, "A gracious good morning to you. Have I reached the person to whom I am speaking?" The person was generally so confused he didn't know how to answer . . . kind of like when people phone the Hill house.

Q: Why does your two-year-old answer the phone?

A: Because he can.

It must simply be impossible to resist the ringing of a phone when you are at that age. Mommy picks it up and, somehow, Daddy is in a little boy's ear moments later. It's magic! *Why not try it myself?* he thinks. *I can do magic too!*

The real magic is that your friends even continue to bother calling once they've run the gauntlet with your two-year-old answering and then his bossy three-year-old sister taking over. The only answer for this is to have calls go straight through to voice mail or run for the phone on the first ring. In our house it gets even funnier. Since the littlest ones learned Spanish as their first language, they pick up the phone, saying, "*Hola! . . . Aye, caramba!*"

> *As a teenager you are at the last stage in your life when you will be happy to hear that the phone is for you.*
>
> —FRAN LEBOWITZ

Phone manners are important for many reasons. Once your children are old enough to reason with, the best way to persuade them to use proper phone etiquette is to explain that when *their* friends call the house, you will answer their phone calls the same way your children answer *your* friends' phone calls. The last thing they want is a parent asking any question other than, "May I please have your name and phone number, and I'll have so-and-so call you back." The thought of you asking their friends, "Why are you calling?" or "Are you his girlfriend? What do you want him for?" makes them shudder with the thought of being banished to the cafeteria table where the kids who bring in Spam sandwiches in Sponge Bob lunch boxes sit. You don't want them asking improper questions of your friends, and they certainly don't want you asking those questions of their friends.

While I always advocate being on top of what is going on in your children's lives, the place to get information is not while answering the phone. Leave it with "Is there any message I can pass on to him or, perhaps, something I can help you with?" Regardless of your offer, their friends will almost always say, "No, that's okay." It's a kid thing.

So how can you teach your children proper phone etiquette without standing next to them each time they pick up the receiver? Leave a list next to the phone, leading the children through the drill step-by-step.

1.   "Hello, this is the Hill residence." Urge them not to substitute *loony bin* for your family name, no matter how much they would like to.

2.   If the phone call is for you, say, "This is he/she." If the caller asks for someone else, respond, "One moment please, and I'll see if he/she is here." Not only is that comment proper, but it has the added benefit of allowing the person being phoned to determine if he or she has time to speak on the phone right then, especially if it is someone known for long conversations, like my sister. Adrienne can turn a one-minute "Is there anything I can pick up for you at the grocery store?" into a thirty-minute explanation of her past experiences at every grocery store in a twenty-mile radius. I love her, but whoa, can she talk! My husband always knows when Adrienne is calling because I settle in, lean back in the chair, and kick up my feet. The clear body language is "It's gonna be a long one."

3.   If the family member isn't available, tell them to take a message. If your kids are like mine, they will need a pen and paper *very* handy since important information for you holds the same place of prominence as remembering their English class vocabulary list from two months ago. Because the thought of moving five feet to open a drawer to find paper seems preposterously difficult to them, I have a magnetic notepad on the refrigerator next to the phone.

4.   If it's still unlikely that a legible message will be taken, I tell them to ask the person to please call back and leave a message on the machine. While this isn't preferable, I think it would be worse not

to get the message, never return the call, and have the caller think you're ignoring her—one more friendship down the tubes!

Tip: we have a high tolerance level for the babblings of young children, but that's not the case with everyone. My mother is frustrated when she calls and has to spend two minutes negotiating with my two-year-old to try to talk him into "getting Mommy" when he would rather wax poetic on going "big boy potty." Try using a toy phone to teach the youngest ones how to answer. You may even get lucky, and they will be content with that until they are able to use proper phone etiquette.

WHAT ABOUT UNCHECKED BEHAVIOR?

From B. G. in Washington, DC:

I work in a store, and one day a boy no more than four or five was at the top of a stairwell, swinging a rolled-up map in a hard plastic tube at a book display. The tube was larger than he was. Books were flying everywhere, and if anyone had been coming up the stairs, the person would have been hit.

His mother was ten feet away, having a conversation but could easily see what he was doing. I went to the boy and told him to stop. I wasn't rude, but I was firm. His mother became furious. She asked how I dared to tell her child what to do. I told her someone had to and that he could have hurt someone. Her response was that she would worry about it if he actually did hurt anyone.

My jaw hit the floor. Seeing that I was getting nowhere, I asked her to keep an eye on her son and walked away. She went to the desk and asked for the manager. I'm the manager. I suggested that she not return to the store if she was unwilling to control her child. It then dawned on me why I had such a close relationship with the juvenile officer at the police department. I was dealing with the effects of this brand of parenting.

> *Adorable children are considered to be the general property*
> *of the human race. Rude children belong to their mothers.*
>
> —JUDITH MARTIN

I'm sure this story doesn't come as a shock to most people. We've all seen poor and even dangerous behavior that goes unchecked. So how do you stop it? How do you change your child's behavior?

Sometimes, you really can change the behavior by ignoring it. If the child is simply seeking attention and doesn't get it, he may stop. However, in the situation highlighted above, behavior that is dangerous to a child or someone else must be stopped immediately.

If the behavior is not dangerous but more annoying, give the silent treatment a shot. This technique becomes more difficult when you have multiple children because even when you ignore it, the other kids may not. One specific issue we had was when J. D. taught Sumner how to make nasty flatulence noises by blowing on her arm. She thought it was very funny, and when he demonstrated how he did it, she was a quick study. This is the time when you wonder why they can't choose to teach something worthwhile such as the alphabet or how to write their names. Miracles do happen but not when there is the chance to pass on the wisdom of how to make a really gross noise.

When Sumner started blowing on her arm, making noises that would make a gastroenterologist blush, we kept a straight face. The other kids didn't. The boys thought this was the funniest thing they'd seen in ages. They couldn't wait to have her do it in front of their friends. The ignore-it-and-it-will-go-away concept didn't work in this case.

We told Sumner she'd get a time-out if she did it again and then told the boys to teach her how to whistle instead. Turns out they got just as much enjoyment out of watching her pucker her lips and spit as she was trying to learn to whistle. The gross part is the part they particularly like. Boys . . .

FOOD FRENZY

We can all think of something we didn't like to do or some food we didn't like to eat. Nothing and no one was going to change it. It's the same for kids today, and that may be one reason for bad manners. I have had several children who come over to play with my kids, and when I serve them lunch, they inform me that they either don't like hot dogs or fish or salad or soup. You name it. I tell my children that when they are at someone else's house, they have to politely refrain from commenting on what they don't like and at least take a nibble of what is offered.

> *The most remarkable thing about my mother is that for thirty years she served the family nothing but leftovers. The original meal has never been found.*
>
> —CALVIN TRILLIN

At home they can't get everything they want, but I do let them in on the selection process. I have always hated eating liver. The look, the smell, and the taste simply disgust me. Even the thought of it would make me truly nauseous. My mother would cook it anyway and tell me that because it provided iron, I had to eat it. I would make excuses to use the restroom and spit it out, and when that trick was figured out, I just sat there at the table, refusing to eat. I would sit there four hours, five hours, as long as it took for my mother to give up and let me go to bed. I now know there are plenty of ways to get iron in my diet, and I think she should have offered choices.

While you aren't going to cook a special meal for each child (and if you do, you are certifiable), it is healthy and helpful to explain good eating habits to kids and let them help select the food for meals based on the healthy eating plan. If they hate broccoli, offer green beans, spinach, or zucchini. If they don't like pork, offer beef, turkey, chicken. We happen to eat fish the majority of evenings. One child loves salmon, and the other hates it but loves tuna.

We alternate and allow the child to eat more of the other dinner items that one day.

I confess that we have also resorted to trickery when a child refuses to even try something that is unfamiliar. Most of the kids are pretty adventurous. They've eaten lamb brains, raw sea urchins split open tableside, the claws of chickens from street vendors in China, and they've never had so much as an upset stomach. However, Wyatt is different. He would gag (for real) at the mention of the word *tomato*. When Joe and I began dating, he was a permissive parent. The kids ruled the roost. They only ate scrambled eggs and ketchup for breakfast. No ketchup? Then no eggs until they got the ketchup. For lunch and dinner they would eat only chicken nuggets and French fries. Wyatt was the worst. He would never deviate from his delicious, dependable habit. It presented a problem because as with most normal kids, when my children saw Joe's children were eating junk food, they wanted it too.

Fortunately, Joe realized he was creating a huge problem and changed his behavior. Jordan and Collin learned to like other foods, but Wyatt was a holdout. Finally, one evening we were at a restaurant that served frog legs. As the cliché goes, "It tastes just like chicken." We ordered them and told him they were little chicken drumsticks. He ate them and liked it. Then we fessed up. While he still doesn't have the most cosmopolitan of palates, he eats much better. Also, keep in mind that any pediatrician will tell you no harm will come to a child who infrequently misses a meal or has an unbalanced meal once in a while.

THE MATURITY ARGUMENT

When your children become a bit older, you may notice that you have a greater problem with them being disrespectful and argumentative with you and others, including teachers and friends. Teens falsely associate becoming an adult with doing what they want, when they want, and how they want. Frequently, attempts to guide them in a certain direction are met with arguments, foul language, and sometimes obscene gestures. While it's true that one of the most important areas of teen development is the establishment of their identity, permissive parents fall into the trap of seeing a more mature-*looking* child and, accordingly, expecting them to *be* more mature. Further, they seem to expect the maturity to spring forth like a new blossom without any planting, watering, or weeding. Remember, nonpermissive parenting is a job, and this is one of the times when it is not that pleasant.

> *The young always have the same problem—how to rebel and conform at the same time. They have now solved this by defying their parents and copying one another.*
>
> —QUENTIN CRISP

Children use socially unacceptable language and are argumentative for a couple of reasons. First, sometimes they are trying to make themselves believe they are tougher than they are. Their idea would be if Mom doesn't approve of my language and I don't care, then I'm stronger. They may associate it (incorrectly) with adult behavior.

Second, they want to test the waters and see what comments are acceptable and which are not. How and whether you react to this behavior will matter a great deal to your relationship with your child. Can you imagine visiting your grandmother and cussing her out? Of course not. Would you feel comfortable talking like a character out of a rap video in front of your own mother? I doubt it. So why do permissive parents allow their own children to talk to them and treat them that way? They are more concerned with being *liked* by their teen than being a parent to their child.

Follow their lazy and faulty reasoning further, and some parents will tell you that when their children speak that way to them and in front of them, it shows how close they are. Nothing is hidden. They're free to be themselves in front of each other without that messy thing called judgment.

Nonpermissive parents teach their children that respect for themselves, their parents, and others means that certain language and behavior are off-limits.

You can have disagreements without it degenerating into swearing and name-calling. You can have discussions that don't reach the decibel level of airplane engines. I don't think a totalitarian approach to this is helpful. You can acknowledge the feelings of your child, saying, "I understand you don't think it's fair that you can't go to the party." At the same time you can stop the uncivil behavior with, "You are not allowed to swear at me."

Finally, add in the consequences. "I am still not going to let you attend the party, and it was a mistake to treat me disrespectfully because there are consequences." Explain what the consequence is for swearing, and stick to it. If you are firm, kids will intelligently come to the conclusion that they are only making the situation worse for themselves by throwing in more uncivil behavior. Appeal to their intelligence. Remember that when they cross the line, you must consistently impose the consequences you have stated.

FINALLY . . .

If teenagers feel it's unnecessary to be respectful to their own parents—the persons who feed them, clothe them, pay for everything they need—why would they think they need to show respect to anyone else? That mother is not raising an independent, self-reliant, resilient teen who will respect his mother for her wise guidance. She is creating a monster.

I can't really say what has caused the decline in civility, politeness, and manners in our country. Of course, the permissive parenting notion, which states that children should have the exact same choices and, frequently, lack of boundaries in life as adults have, is largely to blame, but another culprit is entertainment.

A study at the National Institute of Mental Health found that children who see kindness and good behavior on television imitate it. Numerous studies also show that children who view the opposite imitate that as well. But it's a cop-out to solely blame TV for a child's problems. The parents bought the TV and pay for the cable. They have control and can select programming that educates, inspires, and intrigues their child. Many simply don't.

Parents know manners, civility, empathy, and respect are the cornerstones of their family life and our society. Permissive parents hope their children learn that behavior on their own. Nonpermissive parents accept the time, patience, perseverance, and sometimes disappointments it takes to raise a well-mannered child.

When you are a mother you are never really alone in your thoughts. A mother has to think twice, once for herself and once for her child.

—Sophia Loren

Spanking, Time-Outs, and Other Eight-Letter Words

If you bungle raising your children, I don't think
whatever else you do well matters very much.

—Jacqueline Kennedy Onassis

A twelve-year-old boy in South Carolina was arrested and handcuffed just before Christmas in 2006. Why? His mother discovered that before Christmas he had unwrapped a Nintendo Game Boy Advance, which was a present from his great-grandmother. When his great-grandmother realized it was missing, she told his mother, who asked the boy about it. He claimed ignorance, but after the mother threatened to call the police, the boy admitted he had opened it and taken it to his room.

The mother called the police anyway, saying her son showed no remorse, and she hoped the incident would be a wake-up call for him. This mom needs help! If you ever find yourself ready to call the police because your child has opened a gift early, please seek professional help. The boy needs nonpermissive parenting, not the police.

The dictionary says that *discipline* means "to bring to a state of order and obedience." And *punishment* is "a penalty inflicted for an offense." Why do I need to use dictionary definitions? The permissive-parenting crowd gets squeamish about certain words. One of the ways to achieve discipline is through punishment. Now don't be shocked, but I'm going to use the phrase "punish your child." If you can't handle using the proper word to describe what you're doing, you'll likely not be very effective at administering it either. But a lot of parents don't understand the art of discipline.

TEMPER, TEMPER!

If you're a parent, you've probably experienced toddler and teenager temper tantrums. One isn't worse than the other; they just have to be handled differently. The same thing is true for sassy children, kids who cuss, and the like. I'm not about to say that every child should always be perfectly behaved. It just doesn't happen. I am always a little leery of families where the children never seem to step out of line. It just isn't normal. I always suspect the parents must have strapped electrodes onto the children surreptitiously and threatened to zap them if they made one false move. A kid who misbehaves isn't necessarily a bad child, just one that needs to learn a better way to deal with life's frustrations.

> *The secret of dealing with a child is not to be its parent.*
> —MELL LAZARUS

I also feel that it is important for children to learn to test boundaries and to make mistakes. The greatest lessons in life can come from mistakes you make, if you learn from them. That's the key, and it's the challenge to parents. The goal isn't to stop your child from ever making a mistake or acting out. It's to support good behavior and punish bad behavior so that, as they grow, so does their comprehension, which enables them to start making smarter choices for themselves.

TO SPANK OR NOT TO SPANK?

Thomas Szasz says, "In the United States today, there is a pervasive tendency to treat children as adults and adults as children. The options of children are thus steadily expanded while those of adults are progressively constricted. The result is unruly children and childish adults."[1] And how right he is!

So let's talk about one of the greatest and most controversial parenting debates in my lifetime: spanking. I have become a very different parent with each successive child. There isn't a parent alive who wants to spank a child. We would prefer that our adored and beloved offspring behave, and that on the rare occasions that they don't, they will respond to our rational, calmly stated reasons why they need to change their behavior. But what do you do when your six-year-old takes his truck and smacks it onto your four-year-old's fingers because the littler one made the mistake of touching the truck?

First, you tell him not to do it again. Then he repeats the action with a defiant look at you. As the four-year-old sibling screams nearby, you rationally explain that you know he has intentionally disobeyed you and is deliberately hurting his sibling. You repeat that the sibling didn't mean any harm by touching the truck. You end with "So don't do it again."

He does it again. Welcome to the perplexing world of punishment.

I left the hospital after giving birth to my first child and having (like every obsessive American mother) read at least three parenting books. There was no way I would ever spank my child because I had learned through these illuminating books how to be a perfect parent. My children would love and adore me so much (since all I would ever show them was love and adoration) that they would never behave in a way that was out of line. I remember reading that if you hit your children, they would learn to hit too. Okay. It sounds reasonable. Unfortunately, it must have been written by one of the child psychology experts who was so busy earning a string of educational initials behind his "Dr." title that he didn't have time to raise children.

So later on when my eldest hauled off and bonked a littler one on the hand, I was thrown into territory I hadn't expected. I tried the next step. I removed her from the situation. I picked her up and put her in her bedroom and closed the door. Do you know what she did next? She picked up her little rocking chair with the pretty pink flowers painted on it and held it high above her head and began beating the door. Paint was flying everywhere. The chair rockers made indents the size of large olives in the door. No amount of putty was going to fill those holes! I opened the door, sat her on the bed, and explained that she couldn't behave like this. I told her how much work it would take for me to fix and repaint her door. I left the room.

She picked the rocking chair right back up and went at it again. *OK, Dr. Spock, what do I do now?* I thought. What did I do? I spanked her. But I felt so guilty. I thought about the lifelong scars she might bear because of the spanking. I wondered how I could have failed as a parent so much that I couldn't even keep my three-year-old from acting out. Years and many children later, I realize her actions were fairly normal, and my reaction to spank her was too.

As someone said, "a pat on the back helps develop character if given often enough, early enough, and low enough." So why did I feel so guilty? All of those people who spent years in school studying the psyche of a child and adolescent behavior determined that spanking would ruin a child for life and could make him a psychopathic, violent killer. They said we could just talk to our children as if they were rational adults, and that would change their behavior. Their neat, tidy, and oh-so-smart-sounding answers had one problem. In the real world of parenting, they didn't work.

Dr. Benjamin Spock is often credited (or condemned) for the no-spanking movement. In reality, Dr. Spock never fully ruled out spanking, but his belief that "children were little people" led many to assume that meant young children were individuals whose rights and beliefs must, therefore, be equal with their parents'. Oddly enough, when liberal countries followed the child-rearing-with-no-spanking technique it backfired.

For instance, in 1979 Sweden outlawed spanking by parents. Over the next ten years, reports of serious child abuse increased more than 400 percent. There were no scientific reports indicating that bad childhood behavior had decreased. Had Swedish parents been driven insane by not being able to punish their children as they thought appropriate? Were they fearful the government was going to take away all parenting rights, so they struck back at their children? Perhaps they feared if little children knew so much that a parent didn't need to (and legally couldn't) spank them, why would there be any need for parenting?

Whatever the reason for the inexcusable abuse, the point that was clear was that the government didn't have the answers. Some people theorize it was a left-wing conspiracy to create a nanny state where the government would eventually take over all parental responsibilities. I think the pendulum simply swung too far out and needed to start coming back toward the middle. Americans live in the middle. We are pretty normal, rational people. We don't want the government taking over our jobs and our family roles as it is done in other countries.

> *Your children need your presence more than your presents.*
>
> —JESSE JACKSON

In the early to mid nineties, people started questioning the answers of the seventies. We had been told that spanking children under any circumstances was horrible and that we were bad parents, in fact, parental failures if we couldn't change our children's behavior by simply talking with them. Then someone realized that the majority of adults in America were spanked as youngsters and didn't grow up to be pickax-wielding mass murderers.

In 1996 the director of residential research at Boys Town, which is a spank-free zone, studied 166 children. The conclusions were astounding. They showed that no other discipline technique worked better for children under age thirteen than spanking. But, they warned, spankings must occur in a supportive environment, not an abusive or neglectful one.

A survey by the American Academy of Pediatrics (AAP) now defines *corporal punishment* as "the use of spanking as a form of discipline which *does not* include beating or other actions that might be considered child abuse." The experts realize there is a difference, and it's a huge one, between spanking a child and abusing a child. Nearly all pediatricians recommend parents try nonphysical forms of punishment, but four out of ten say if that doesn't work, they recommend corporal punishment with specific rules and conditions as an effective form of discipline.

What do the experts do? Some 35 percent spank their own children according to that AAP Periodic Survey.[2] That doesn't mean everyone should run out and find a child to spank. And there's never, ever a reason to spank or in any way do something painful to an infant. It simply means that spanking in an appropriate circumstance can be effective instead of life damaging.

CHILD ABUSE

There is no set definition of *child abuse* nationwide. It's hard to explain it, but you know it when you see it. It can come in several forms, including physical, emotional, and verbal abuse. The results are devastating. We generally focus on physical abuse, but think of the verbal abuse you see much more frequently. I was at a tiny, one-lift ski hill, dropping off the children. The mother in front of me also had little kids. They were moving slowly and complaining about the cold. She started cursing at them and about them. I can't begin to cover the words she used.

> *Children seldom misquote. In fact, they usually repeat*
> *word for word what you shouldn't have said.*
>
> —AUTHOR UNKNOWN

I actually walked up to them and said, "I am so sorry that your mother has to use this kind of language because she doesn't have a large enough vocabulary to express what she wants to say."

Her mouth just dropped open. But what could she say? All the curse words in the world don't explain to your child why their behavior is bad. Meanwhile, they are verbally abusive to a child. Those types of words don't express anything except your own frustration. They are a cop-out used so that adults can vent their frustration, instead of having to find the language to express what they really need to say. What lesson does that teach children? Children identify with their parents, so verbal abuse by their parents becomes a way in which they see themselves, and that's abusive in itself. As someone said, "Children are natural mimics, who act like their parents despite every effort to teach them good manners."

I ran across an article on the Web site imperfectparent.com, which accomplished the rare feat of being funny, sad, and true. The author, Michelle O'Neil, uses a backward way of addressing this issue—she *facetiously* embraces it.

Let the cuss words fly wherever and whenever you please. Kids will pick up on this and start swearing on their own. Watch their little shoulders drop and the tension leave their bodies with each resounding expletive. It's not only cute, it is therapeutic! Strap them in the back seat, make sure they're tired and hungry, and then venture out into rush-hour traffic. Inevitably, someone will cut you off. Between the other drivers and the kids whining and complaining, you're sure to slip. After your first time, it just gets easier and easier to go with the potty mouth flow. Of course, children will need to be instructed that some people don't like swearing. Teach them to weigh the health benefits vs. the repercussions of getting kicked out of the Boy Scouts, Sunday school, and the like. Consider this a learning opportunity, a chance for your little angel to experience choices and the consequences of their actions. Sure, some namby-pamby kids might opt to go all goodie two shoes, but with constant support from parents, your child will eventually learn how to swear. Of course, Grandma won't like it, but $#*%@ to her! She could use a little cuss therapy herself.[3]

As Albert Schweitzer said, "Adults teach children in three important ways: The first is by example, the second is by example, and the third is by example." The reality is that your language, just like emotional and physical abuse, has a lasting impact, whether you intend it or not. Abused children have a multitude of issues that will make your job as a parent harder instead of easier. That type of punishment hurts the child, the family, and our society. The American Academy of Child and Adolescent Psychiatry (AACAP) reports that children who have been abused may display these traits:

- a poor self-image
- sexual acting out
- inability to trust or love others
- aggressive, disruptive, and sometimes illegal behavior
- anger and rage
- self-destructive or self-abusive behavior, suicidal thoughts
- passive, withdrawn, or clingy behavior
- fear of entering into new relationships or activities
- anxiety and fears
- school problems or failure
- feelings of sadness or other symptoms of depression
- flashbacks, nightmares
- drug and alcohol abuse
- sleep problems

Further, the AACAP reports that many abused children become parents who abuse their own children. The problems go even further because their studies show that abused children have trouble as adults establishing intimate personal relationships and develop psychological issues with physical closeness, touching, intimacy, and trust. In terms of their own medical issues, they have a higher rate of anxiety, depression, substance abuse, medical illness, and work problems.[4] I certainly don't want any of that for my kids, and I'm sure you don't want it for yours either. We've probably all had brushes with kids who were likely abused.

There was a boy in my high school class who came to school with a black eye and bruises a number of times. Nowadays I'm sure the school administration would immediately contact Child Protective Services. Back then, people just didn't talk about it. He wouldn't speak about what happened, but another one of the boys, who lived on a nearby ranch, knew what went on. His dad had a drinking problem, and whenever his son did anything out of line, he was beaten. Not spanked but beaten with fists.

It's hard to imagine this boy doing much wrong. He was well-behaved, extremely polite, and studied hard, but, apparently, it didn't take much to get his dad going. The result was that the boy rarely invited people over, and although he was a good athlete and well liked, he kept to himself and never really became close to many people. He always seemed a little leery. As we got older, I wondered what kind of spouse and parent he would become. It turned out that he married a quiet, lovely girl from the grade below us. He remained kind, quiet, and sober. Nonpermissive parenting is not abusive parenting.

The heightened awareness of abuse is a good development and has changed forms of punishment which were wrongly accepted. In my high school, students were whipped with a leather strap for infractions as minor as touching the gym floor with their street shoes. At home we were whipped with a strap, too, usually a belt. My feeling is that when you feel the need to use something other than your hand to spank, the spanking could easily cross the line to abuse. Yes, kids get too big to spank with your hand. But by that time, they are old enough for other forms of punishment that likely will be much more effective. Remember, the focus is not on *hurting* a child but on *changing a child's behavior* to help him become a better adult.

DISCIPLINE STAGES

Let's go through some stages. If a child is old enough to know right from wrong and to listen to a simple line of reasoning, and he continues to disobey, what is the solution? Each child and each family is different and what works for one may not work for another. Here are some stories of mine and others that have been shared with me.

> *You can learn many things from children.*
> *How much patience you have, for instance.*
> —FRANKLIN P. JONES

From L. T. in Texas:

I raised four kids and when they did misbehave from time to time I applied the "Board of Education" to the "Seat of Learning." Today all are good, productive, loving adults. I drove foolishness from them firmly, not abusively, and today I don't have a bunch of fools for children.

The key phrase she uses is "not abusively." That signals that she realizes it is easily possible to go over the line.

In the *Journal of Applied Developmental Psychology*, Dr. Paul Frick, a psychologist at the University of New Orleans, wrote about the study he conducted of ninety-eight children. Dr. Frick suggests parents push spanking to the back of the line and try to use other types of discipline first, such as time-out, extra chores, and loss of privileges. Each of the children he studied showed negative effects from physical punishment—and didn't learn what the parents were trying to teach. Spanking, when you use it, has to be coupled with an explanation of why the spanking was necessary and what behavior the child needs to change for his own positive development.[5]

> *Even when freshly washed and relieved of all obvious confections, children tend to be sticky.*
>
> —FRAN LEBOWITZ

Last weekend my three-year-old, who had been watching me cook dinner, decided to turn the stove on himself and check out the pretty flames. Fortunately, I turned back to the stove while his hand was on the way to the fire. I slapped it, and he jumped back. His lower lip immediately moved into a jaw-to-jaw quivering frown as he got ready to wail.

I immediately started talking to him. I asked him if the smack hurt, and he nodded yes. I told him I wasn't mad at him but that I didn't want him to touch something that was dangerous and would hurt him much, much more. I asked him if he wanted to burn his hand. Of course, he shook his head no. I told him the fire was hot, and it would burn him and could cause a bigger fire. Finally, I said that he was not allowed to touch the stove at any time. While I certainly had the option of grabbing him and pulling him back from the flame, I know that by smacking his hand and then talking to him, he got a message he will remember.

I wouldn't have to do the same thing with my four-year-old. By simply talking sharply to her, she would begin the lip trembling and would remember not to do it again. So here is my two cents' worth of advice. If a two-year-old child dashes off a sidewalk and into a street, I will give him a swat because his action can result in death. At that young an age, it's impossible to rationally explain to the child the lifelong consequences, which would require him to understand the whole life cycle just to comprehend. Two-year-olds need to instinctively know not to run into the street because Mom or Dad will swat them. After they're a bit older, you can do all the explaining and reasoning you want.

Ditto for kids like my little guy who grab at items on the stove. A hand swat, fast and simple, generally keeps them from trying it again. Some children learn it quickly, others need a couple of swats, but aside from keeping them in a straitjacket in their bedrooms, it's the best solution I've come up with for that age group. I have noticed that there are some good children's books and programs with stories that help teach children the same lesson, and those are probably a great thing to share with kids. But at an early age, if there is a dangerous action, the hand swat is my first reaction with a sharp, "No!"

From J. B. in Tennessee:

My children and I were in Dillard's in Memphis, Tennessee, when two of them began throwing fits about going to look at toys in another store. They were yelling and carrying on. I swept them up, spanked their rears, and dared anyone to object. It was as simple as that.

If there were no schools to take children away from home part of the time, the insane asylums would be filled with mothers.

—EDGAR W. HOWE

From M. L. in South Carolina:

My son decided to talk very loudly during prayer one Sunday. I swooped him up in an under-arm carry like a football and marched out the center aisle as he yelled, "Help me! Help me!" the whole way. I have my doctorate in education and believe discipline has two aspects: logical consequence and immediate accountability and responsibility.

I think M. L. hits the nail right on the head. Punishment should logically fit the crime and occur sooner versus later. If your child decides to play tug-o-war with the dog, using his sister's favorite doll, what discipline logically fits the crime? Sure, the sister could give the dog the brother's favorite car to chew, but since the boy clearly likes playing with the dog, it's probably more effective to ban the brother from playing with the dog for a certain period of time. There needs to be good reasoning behind any discipline unless a child is too young to understand logical consequences.

TIME-OUT

The time-out is one of those creations from the 1970s. It can work but not at every age and not for every child. Put yourself in the place of a child. You know you're not supposed to eat candy before dinner, but you sneak a piece from the cupboard and eat it anyway. Your mom catches you and gives you a time-out.

> *Better a little chiding than a great deal of heartbreak.*
> —WILLIAM SHAKESPEARE

Now, I know that one of my kids would absolutely be willing to have the candy and take the time-out every day. He doesn't mind sitting there for a while, because he's made the determination that eating the yummy candy is worth a ten-minute time-out. That leads a child to determine what behavior is worth a time-out. When that happens, you aren't changing the behavior; instead, you're teaching the child to evaluate risks versus rewards. Keep in mind, your job is to instill in your child a belief, behavior, and value system that will lead him to become a good, productive adult. The time-out logic can be easily misunderstood. As a teen or adult he might use the same logic: *should I cheat on the test and risk the small chance of getting caught? What is that A worth? Is stealing a camera worth six months in jail? How much do I want that camera?* He needs to make behavior choices based on right and wrong.

Further, I know a lot of parents who give children time-outs in their bedrooms. Have you taken a good look at a kid's bedroom lately? My kids have their Game Boys, their toys, Nerf mini basketball hoops, and all kinds of other things. My childhood bedroom was stocked with my favorite books. Spending time in my room was no biggie. Sure, you can go into the room and remove any item that looks like it might be fun for the period of the time-out and then put it back, but that seems to be punishing you more than the child. The bottom line is if you choose to use time-outs, make sure they matter. Here are a few good ideas from smart parents:

From R. M. in Mississippi:
When our children were toddlers we employed a time-out chair. Instead of simply having them sit there, we made them count to one hundred or recite the ABCs.

From D. G. in Tennessee:
In our house we, too, have a time-out chair. The chair is in the middle of the kitchen where there is no TV, no toys, and no games. It is boring and it works.

From A. J. in Texas:
When the kids don't listen, and I have to call them more than once, I have them crack open a book to read or fill out educational workbooks (that one is a real winner with them!). We don't have any cable, direct or satellite TV, so I sometimes take away an hour of TV.

They usually only have one show they really want to watch, and that is the hour that they have to miss.

A time-out can work for younger children but only if it truly removes them from a fun environment and forces them to do something they dislike so much that they will change their behavior.

THE SHARING STRUGGLE

Sharing is one of the toughest lessons for a toddler to learn. In fact, they have their own set of rules about it:

> Toddler's Rules of Ownership
> *If I like it, it's mine.*
> *If it's in my hand, it's mine.*
> *If I can take it from you, it's mine.*
> *If I had it a little while ago, it's mine.*
> *If it's mine, it must never appear*
> *to be yours in any way.*
> *If I'm doing or building something,*
> *all the pieces are mine.*
> *If it looks just like mine, it's mine.*
> *If I think it's mine, it's mine.*
> —Author Unknown

Although I don't know where this originated, I do know that it's 100 percent accurate. Remember how much you used to like to share things when you were a kid? You didn't. No child likes to share, especially a toddler. This list represents a child's ultimate fantasy world. You create the reality. At first I tried reasoning with my little ones. Hello! You can't reason with a toddler! I know. I realize that . . . now.

Here is the dialogue:

Me: You can alternate playing with your brother's Dancing Elmo. Wolf
    is going to play with him for two minutes, and then it's your turn.

Here is what goes through a toddler's mind:

Sumner: *What is two minutes? What do you mean alternate? If it's out
    of my hand, it's gone, and I want it back . . . now!*

Here's what works for me even at the toddler level:

If Sumner takes something from Wolf, then I let Wolf take some-
    thing of Sumner's.

Me: If you want his Dancing Elmo, then Wolf can take your Pretty
    Pet Pony.

Sumner: *Hmmm. This is interesting, and I'm not sure I like it. I have the
    Dancing Elmo, but now he has my Pretty Pony. I want that too.*

If she takes her Pony back, then I give Elmo back to Wolf. You can use
whatever language you want to accompany this exchange process, but it's
going through the changeover several times that makes the point. They catch
on and almost always decide they'd rather keep their own items than have
someone else touch their toys even if that means they can't have all the things
they want. By two and a half or three, they get the basic idea of what is fair.
That doesn't mean they like it, but if you use that as a basis for your actions,
they get it.

Sharing can be difficult for children and often brings out deviousness. My
sister, Adrienne, loves ice cream. Really, really loves it. One afternoon in our
elementary school years, we wanted to have some ice cream when we arrived
home. I got to the freezer first and scooped a heaping bowl, leaving very little
for her. Yes, I know it wasn't my finest hour in the sharing department.

When I turned my back to take a spoon out of the drawer and to get
the chocolate syrup from the cabinet, she figured she'd show me. While she
couldn't simply take the ice cream or switch bowls because I'd take it right
back, she could make it so that I didn't want to eat the ice cream. She pulled
out the salt shaker and shook it all over my ice cream! Then she went back to
the table and waited. My ice cream looked great. I had added the chocolate
sauce from the Hershey's can, which was absolutely heavenly, onto my ice

cream, and I simply knew it was going to be scrumptious. I took a bite and howled for our mother.

My mother punished me for being greedy by not letting me eat any ice cream for a week, and in seconds, she cooked up the ultimate punishment for Adrienne. She had to eat my ice cream. It was awful. I think it scarred her for life!

From M. R. in Pennsylvania:

I figured out a way to keep my two boys from fighting. After one battle I let each of them choose the punishment for the other. They thought about what would be the worst thing for their brother to deal with which, of course, meant it was something they wouldn't like done to them. The punishment the one chose for the other became his own punishment. The fighting stopped.

From V. S. in New Mexico:

My girls used to fight like cats and dogs. You know how pre-teen girls can get! It was vicious. After a day-long ongoing argument I'd had enough. I made them hold each other's hand and go walk around out-side. They thought they looked silly and they were right. They both got so mad at me that they began to actually get along. A common enemy unites most people!

TANTRUMS AND MELTDOWNS

Let's move to the next battlefield. Which of us hasn't had a toddler meltdown in a store? They usually appear out of nowhere and always at the least convenient time, such as when you're juggling egg cartons, zucchini squash, and ice cream tubs. Children with strong bones and healthy bodies turn weak-kneed and drop to the floor of the store as they begin to whine and sob. Often it's because they simply can't survive without the gum, toy, or candy in front of them. Or they may simply want to leave the store. Sumner, my four-year-old, recently dropped to the ground.

Me: What's wrong?
Sumner: My legs are broken.
Me: Why are they broken?
Sumner: Because they want to go home.

Like fruit, children are sweetest just before they turn bad.

—DENA GROQUET

No, it doesn't make sense. Yes, it's easy to give in. You could say that you'll leave right away if only they'll stand up, but as soon as they realize you can't leave immediately, they drop back down. You can give them the candy they're yelling for, but they'll yell again for the next item they see and want. Be strong! The worst thing I see is when permissive parents give in.

You'll hear them say to a three-year-old, "Okay, you can have this half-pound bag of Skittles now but only this time."

Sure. You know very well that the kid is going to be screaming for Skittles the next time down the aisle too. Why? Mom will give in like a sheep ready to be fleeced. Yes, giving in is convenient and pacifies them for a short period of time, but the lesson is wrong, and it will lead them to resort to the same behavior over and over until it becomes almost impossible to change.

From S. J. in Maryland:

When one of my toddlers decided to throw a tantrum in a store I just walked away and left him kicking on the floor. It took him about a nanosecond to realize that I was not taking the bait, and he got up and followed me. It was a little bit embarrassing for the moment but, fortunately, it worked. I did the same thing at home and none of my four kids stayed in the tantrum phase for very long. They learned they won't get attention that way.

I gave S. J.'s method a try. Keep in mind that it takes thirty minutes at the minimum for us to get from our cabin in Texas to anyplace that sells much of anything except for cattle and horse feed. When we go to town, we have a big list, and we're not leaving until it's all checked off. I don't enjoy driving into and out of the city.

We were at Target and needed food, new socks, grilling utensils, and a wastebasket for our bathroom. That wastebasket was a tough one to find. They all seem so fancy. I didn't want one with anything special on it, just something copper or brass colored and plain. I looked and looked. Wolf took one look at the newest aisle I was heading down and did the floor drop. It kind of resembles a grunt when the sergeant tells him to drop and give him twenty, except Wolf didn't do anything but lie there. I put Sheila's plan into motion.

I said, "Well, I have to go to the next aisle," and I did.

Wolf didn't follow. So I loudly announced I was moving down another aisle and did. Then I spotted him up and moving to the aisle. The moment he realized I saw him, he dropped to the floor, this time making lovely snow angel movements and whining. We continued this for a while longer until I realized that finding the wastebasket would waste the whole day. Instead, I picked him up and told him that if he couldn't act like a big boy, then he would have to sit in the baby seat in the cart, and I strapped him in. He did not like that one bit and started to cry. I let him do that a bit and then explained that he could only get out if he was going to walk with me properly. He did.

Surprisingly, while the initial tactic didn't work in the store, it did work at home. When he started fussing, I put him in another room and told him he could fuss as much as he wanted in there. Since I couldn't see him fuss, it didn't do him any good, and he stopped.

I like what *Reader's Digest* had to say: "Words to the Wise: If you have a headache, do what it says on the aspirin bottle: take two, and keep away from children." Honestly, though, shopping with kids can become ridiculous if you don't nip it in the bud.

My sister has an even lower tolerance for whining and pleading. She uses her Dairy Queen Method. It helps to understand that there is something genetic in our family that makes us start twitching with anticipation anytime we are near a DQ. My husband is simply pathetic when it comes to dipped cones. He used to disappear for an hour on weekend mornings. I never saw him leave; he'd just sneak out when I wasn't looking. He'd usually come back with something from town that really wasn't that critical. One time he came home but left whatever he'd bought in the car, so I went out to get it. I found the evidence! There were DQ napkins, an ice cream cone wrapper, and an empty iced tea cup. Now he just tells me up front that he needs a DQ fix.

Anyway, Adrienne realizes shopping is not a child's favorite activity (unless it is for toys), so she tries to make time for treats at the end as a reward for good behavior. They lose that privilege if they whine and beg for everything they see. Further, if she has to say no too many times, she will dock them a future treat. It can be a very powerful lesson for children to watch their family eating Blizzards at Dairy Queen while they sit with a glass of water! If you recognize that your children are forced to spend a significant amount of time doing something that is really, truly boring to them, I don't see any issue with infrequently giving them some kind of a reward, but don't go overboard.

THE BEDTIME BATTLE

Robert Gallagher says, "Anyone who thinks the art of conversation is dead ought to tell a child to go to bed." He's right. There are very few young children who joyfully anticipate bedtime. Frequently, older siblings or Mom and Dad are still up, and that means something is going on they are missing. One doctor recommended I tell my children that if they go to bed on time, each evening I would give them a reward. Doesn't that teach a child that they should get a reward for simply following family rules, which are intended for their own good? This was more "expert" advice that I learned was wisest *not* to follow. Bedtime was not an easy time for us. Telling them to go to bed didn't always work, so we would put them to bed. Ruth Freathy defined the process this way: "Outfoxing the kids = child slycology."

During the day, Matt had a typical eleven-year-old attitude that said, "Don't hug me in public, and certainly don't call me *Sweetie Pie* in front of my friends," but he turned into a snuggle bug at bedtime. He wanted me to sit with him for ages. I had to make a rule that I would stay in their room until they finished their prayers. Matt is creative, and if there is a loophole, he will find it.

Monday night was the regular prayer. Tuesday night he decided to also pray for his friends and teachers. Wednesday night he added prayers for all of our family members, including cousins. Friday was his pièce de résistance! I became leery when he added a prayer for New York Giants player Tiki Barber. Next he prayed for Vince Young, the graduating quarterback for the University of Texas. Finally, he decided to pray for the members of the Tennessee Titans football team . . . individually. I say *finally* because at this point, my husband broke our huddle. As Red Skelton used to say, "Any kid will run an errand for you if you ask at bedtime."

The key to getting kids to go to bed is to give them a five-minute notice, take them to their bedrooms if they don't want to go on their own, do whatever your ritual is, and then leave. Wash. Rinse. Repeat. That's right—if they come out of their rooms just take them right back and lovingly but firmly say "Good night." Eventually, they will realize the rule isn't going to change, and they'll go to bed on their own and stay there. By the way, every child, including teenagers, needs at least eight hours of sleep, and some need closer to nine-and-a-half hours. I think part of teen crankiness is due to lack of sleep.

PICK UP, CLEAN UP

We find that when you want your kids to pick up their toys, it's helpful to use transition statements. For instance, say, "In five minutes you'll need to put away your books and go to bed," which gives your children time to do what they need to and mentally adjust to the fact that bedtime is almost there.

> *Cleaning your house while your kids are still growing up is like shoveling the walk before it stops snowing.*
>
> —Phyllis Diller

Some people suggest having a physical reward, such as a toy, for children who do what they are supposed to. I don't believe they should be rewarded for doing the basics. Rewards should be for behavior above and beyond the norm, not for the expected. We don't set bedtimes by pulling a magical time out of the sky. Bedtimes are set so that children get a healthy amount of rest each night. That should be the reason they follow your direction. You have talked to their doctor, you have read the books, and you are in charge of teaching them what they will need to do for themselves later in life. I know it sounds great, but a lot of times it just doesn't work. Stronger tactics may be called for.

Our children, like most, are not the neatest creatures to roam the earth. It's as if they took *Hansel and Gretel* too much to heart and are afraid that if they don't leave a trail of clothing and personal belongings from their bedroom to the kitchen, out the door, and over the lawn, they will never find their way back. And it got to be too much.

I heard about something California governor Arnold Schwarzenegger does at his house. When the children leave clothes on the floor, he picks them up and throws them away. I'm too frugal to do that, but I tried a variation. I put everything that was left lying about in a large black trash bag. When the kids wanted it, they had to buy it back for a dollar. It didn't entirely rectify the problem, but things have gotten better.

MIMICKING THE MAD

From G. P. in Nevada:

My five-year-old son can't stand still. He is in constant motion, so the worst punishment for him is to make him not move. When he misbehaves I make him stand with his nose against the wall.

From B. L. in Missouri:

This is my foolproof method for stopping kids who are throwing a temper tantrum. As soon as a child starts doing whatever it is, during the fit I explain that they are doing it incorrectly. If they are yelling, I explain that they are yelling wrong and then show them how to yell properly. No matter what they come back with, I tell them it is not quite right. I explain that down to the smallest detail it is important not to mess up a tantrum. If they are on the floor, I explain that their arms and legs have to go out at the same time or else they won't have the right balance. *Don't* try to make sense. Remember you're dealing with a toddler. If they are thinking about what to do next, I find they stop the tantrum. I guess kids can't multitask very well at that age. I used this method for my child and countless others, and it normally isn't necessary to do it twice.

I like Bill's spunk. I'm not sure how many adults are willing to look ridiculous, but I don't mind, so I gave it a shot. I didn't have any success when I tried that with my toddlers. Mimicking them just made them angrier until they had worked themselves up so much that it was an hour before they could calm down. Surprisingly, though, it had the perfect effect with my eleven-year-old son and fifteen-year-old daughter.

> The real menace in dealing with a five-year-old is that in no time at all you begin to sound like a five-year-old.
> —JOAN KERR

J. D. was upset that he couldn't find a game. He's in the middle of a growth spurt, and I'm fairly convinced that the growth in his body has squeezed his brain. He can't find anything these days, and normally he is the most organized of the bunch. He was convinced one of his brothers had hidden it. I mimicked his illogical claim in a very whiny voice, and he started laughing. As soon as that happened, the issue was over.

Laurel was going on about how "simply everybody" had whatever clothing item she wanted. In my best Valley Girl voice, I talked about all the items *every* girl needed and why it was absolutely a life-or-death situation. She realized the absurdity of it and let it go. In both cases, I was able to alleviate the tension and helped them realize their complaints were unnecessary. At this age, stopping their behavior that exact moment is almost secondary to them understanding why it shouldn't start in the first place and keeping it from happening again.

From P. T. in Florida:

When my kids had fits in a store I would set all my stuff down, then ask people next to me to please look at my children, because this was a very rare sight. I would then pull out a camera and begin taking pictures of the kids. First, they were embarrassed by the attention from people they didn't know and, later, they were embarrassed seeing pictures of how they looked when they were throwing fits. Each time they acted up I pulled out the camera. The fit stopped very quickly.

This is also one way to take more pictures of the kids for your photo albums!

From S. S. in Connecticut:

My children are at that questioning age. When I tell them to stop some activity they're doing, such as wiping squished banana on the cat—nice kitty kitty—they ask, "Why?" Yes, it should be obvious, but by asking questions they think they can prolong whatever they're doing before you make them stop. So I simply tell them that I am the boss and that when they get older they can tell me what to do, but until then I'm in charge. The younger ones don't really think it through; it sounds pretty reasonable, so they go along with it.

STEALING: FACING THE MUSIC

At some point most parents will have to deal with a child taking something that does not belong to him. Hopefully, it will happen at an early age, and by properly dealing with it then, you won't have to face it again.

From J. P. in Minnesota:

One time my five-year-old daughter and I arrived home from a store, and she pulled out something we clearly hadn't bought. I marched her right back to the store, despite her teary eyes and found the manager. I had my daughter ask for forgiveness for taking the item. She was devastated, but the lesson was learned and reinforced by the lesson from Exodus 20:15: "Thou shalt not steal." It was a good opportunity at an early age to teach about honesty and repercussions.

I'm ashamed to say that I did the exact same thing at the same age. I took a small hand notebook from Mr. Anderson's general store. When I got home I showed it to my dad, and he asked where it came from. He, too, marched me back to the store and made me return it and apologize. It made a lasting impression.

Later it helped me realize something about children. Kids want to be good. Sometimes they aren't, but even then they do things to let you know they've done something wrong. They want you to know so that you can help them understand what they're doing, why they're doing it, and whether it's right or wrong. You're helping them determine the difference between good and bad behavior. If you ignore a problem or say, "Just don't do it again," children don't learn from their actions. They need to own up to what they've done, apologize, and then, after discussing why the behavior was wrong, promise not to do it again. I think it's always best if children know what the punishment will be for an infraction. Sometimes, though, it's hard to imagine what they might do next.

From G. F. in Delaware:

We find that it works best if you don't feel as if you have to come up with the exact punishment at the time of the infraction. We simply tell our child there will be a consequence for whatever the problem was. Say he was disrespectful on Tuesday. We'd simply say, "You have lost a privilege." He stews about it for a couple days.

On Friday when he wants to sleep over at his best friend's house, we apply the punishment. He can't go. The beauty of this method is that the punishment is meaningful, and you're not forced to quickly think of a punishment that you may later regret.

LEARNING ABOUT LYING

Here is a problem I didn't expect. Yesterday, I returned from a few days away and started catching up on bills. I opened the phone bill and couldn't figure out why it was so much higher than normal. Then I looked more carefully. Someone had called a 900 number four times, and I was charged seven dollars each time. Two of the calls were made in only a minute of each other.

My first thought was that one of the older boys had called a dirty talk phone line. Nope, I called the phone company and found out the calls were made to get an activation code for the online game called *Runescape*. So I called that company and learned a lot. They have a free section for games and a pay section for games that kids pay for monthly by calling to get an activation code. That's what one of the kids had done. Why did he need to call twice in a row? Because it's very difficult for kids to write down the long activation code fast enough. They're almost forced to call back to get the numbers again, and each time they do, they're charged another seven dollars. The company limits the "activation call" attempts to three a month—just few enough so that parents won't get a phone bill showing a huge spike, tipping them off to carefully inspect their bills and figure out what the kids are up to. My bill happened to span June and July, so there were more than three charges, which is why I noticed it.

Next, I looked at the calendar to figure out which kids were around on that day and at the time of the calls. It turned out that it was one of my sister's kids who was in town for football camp. He had activated the code in the past using his dad's phone line because he knew my sister would see it immediately. While at my house, he figured he'd give it a try since I might not notice it either. When my sister quizzed him, he first denied it; then he said he'd called once; next he said he'd called four times but only was able to write the code down once.

Finally, he said he didn't know it was a pay service (even though you clearly have to go to a pay section of the game site to get to it) and said he'd lied about his age because he didn't think the rule that you have to be thirteen years old to play really mattered. You get the idea.

This is a child with the eyes of an angel—wide, round, innocent. He's used them well, but they didn't work this time. My sister was furious at him, but it offered her a great opportunity to talk to him about a lot of things, such as lying, inappropriate Web sites, and charging anything to someone else. My sister is making him do extra chores around the house to earn the money to repay me. She says he's worried that I don't like him anymore. Of course, I do. No child is perfect, and when children err, we are able to use that experience to help them learn correct behavior or to reinforce what they already know but sometimes conveniently forget.

THE WORK DETAIL

Edgar Bergan once joked, "Hard work never killed anybody, but why take the chance?" And my sister agrees with him. Her philosophy is that if children have time to get in any kind of trouble at all, they must have far too much free time on their hands. What to do about it had been a problem. With six children, she was in constant motion trying to keep her home clean, dishes and laundry done, and meals and school lunches made, on top of the task of just being Mom and overseeing homework, paying bills, and keeping track of the finances. Fortunately, she was able to stop working after their fourth child, so that took her own business workload out of the equation.

One day she was at her wits' end and called my mom for mental support. Now, my mother has always had the same solution for dealing with unruly children: "They must be tired; have them take a nap." This time, though, she offered another solution. She said that the kids needed to help out more now that they were old enough. From that point on my sister's new system took shape. She is now one of the most disciplined parents I know. My kids are on best behavior around her because she is a taskmaster.

One of our older boys, Matt, was staying at Adrienne's house last summer. She told Matt and two of her boys to sweep and mop the kitchen floor. Matt is a boy with a premature predilection for an upper management position later in life. He told his two younger cousins that he was going to organize the job. Matt had one boy start sweeping and the other boy to follow the first with the mop.

When Uncle Ron walked in and asked what was going on, Matt explained that he was the manager, and his job was to oversee his workers to make sure they cleaned thoroughly and finished the job. Uncle Ron, who is a pilot and union manager, played along. He explained to Matt that, as a manager, he needed to realize that there are times employees don't show up. In order for Matt to get true management experience, he needed to learn how to do the other employees' jobs so that he could cover for them in case one was absent. Well, it was impossible for Matt to argue with that line of reasoning, and he ended up cleaning the kitchen floor by himself. He hasn't used that line since.

POSITIVE PEER PRESSURE

A number of teachers use this next method, and if you have more than two children, there might be just enough peer pressure for it to work in your home. It's called the Sink-as-a-Class Method. You come up with a fun activity, but for the family to do it, they must earn enough positive points. Positive points are earned by doing things that are above and beyond the call of duty. On the flip side, if any child does something especially naughty, then the tote board gets a negative point. There is peer pressure on the children to behave and work together to achieve a common goal.

From C. V. in Louisiana:

My children love to go to Dunkin Donuts and the aquarium. In order for them to go they have to earn credits. I have plus signs and minus signs with Velcro on the back. If a child does something properly a plus sign gets stuck onto a large board I made. A negative sign goes up and negates the plus sign when they misbehave. They have to collect enough plus signs for each activity they want to do. It is an easy way for younger children to visualize the ramifications of their behavior. I also think it is equally important to recognize good behavior as well as bad behavior.

> *No pressure, no diamonds.*
>
> —MARY CASE

From K. T. in Ohio:

We have a six-year-old son who is very much into playing sports. He's usually a very well behaved child; but he's picked up the bad habit of mimicking me when I tell him to do something. Or he'll even just say no to me. I told him a few weeks ago that each time he did that he would have to skip baseball for the day. So far it's working!

A much-anticipated event such as a trip to a theme park or a ball game is also a huge carrot to hold in front of a child. The problem is that it's a tough one for parents to uphold. If you tell your child that you won't take him to the ball game with you unless he cleans his room, then he'd better only be at the ball game if the room is clean. Unfortunately, that punishes parents, too, since they want to be experiencing these events with their children. Often that's why we've planned them in the first place. Do not say, "This hurts me as much as it hurts you." You haven't done anything wrong, and they'll think you're stupid for punishing yourself needlessly. Further, the issue isn't about you and your feelings; it's about them and their actions. Don't confuse things. Stick to what you say or don't say it.

DON'T SLAM THAT DOOR!

Henny Youngman once quipped, "What is a home without children? Quiet." That's funny . . . but some noises kids make are not, such as door slamming.

From R. M. in California:

My daughter got into the habit of going to her room and slamming the door whenever she didn't get her way and was angry. One day, after storming off to her room and slamming the door, I informed her that, if she did it again, she wouldn't have a door to slam. Of course, the door slammed behind me when I left. I returned a minute later with a screwdriver, removed the door, and took it with me. After a door-less week, I put it back on, and it hasn't slammed since.

From A. R. in Kansas:

My son was seven, and I reprimanded him for something, so he ran off to his room and slammed the door. I told him that, if he did it again, there would be consequences. A week later, after an outing didn't go the way he wanted, he did it again. I got a screwdriver and a hammer and went upstairs without speaking to him at all and set about taking the door off its hinges. My son demanded to know what I was doing. I told him that since he wasn't treating the door properly, he wasn't allowed to have it.

He yelled, "You can't do that!"

To which I replied, "Just watch me."

I kept the door for a few days and then returned it to its proper place. I haven't had the problem again.

Door slamming didn't bother me too much at first. I figured it was a loud but relatively easy way for the kids to blow off some steam. But after a while door slamming began to reach the level of an art form, especially for our girls. They would pause in the doorway, dramatically swish their arm back, and slam the door with such force the windows would shake. Our house is eighty-one years old. The doors have been painted and repainted so many times that the door slams would actually knock slabs of paint off anything within tremor distance. It had to stop.

I did the same thing A. R. and R. M. did. Laurel slammed her door, and I told her the door would come off if she slammed it again. She did, so

I promptly took off the door when she left for school. I moved the door into the hallway and pocketed the hinges. I recommend taking it off while they are out of the house. The impact of a room with no door is greater when it just hits them all at once.

At first Laurel tried propping the door against the frame. It became tiresome to move it back and forth each time she walked in and out, so she gave up on that one. Her brothers took full advantage of the situation to bother her. They would walk very slowly back and forth in front of her door and make comments about the room. It drove her nuts.

The next time she blew up, there was no bedroom door to slam, so she slammed her bathroom door. Guess what? I took that one off too. Teenage girls love privacy. No bedroom door, no bathroom door, no privacy. She took towels and taped them up over the door frames, but that didn't work very well either since she could still hear her brothers' comments, along with the fact that the tape kept coming off, causing the towels to fall down.

Finally, she gave in and promised not to slam the door again. It took almost a month. The girl has a strong will, but the desire for a door was stronger. It's been two years now, and she hasn't slammed a door again. Further, the very first time her brothers slammed their doors, I told them that if they did it again, the same punishment was in their future. They knew I meant it, so they stopped immediately.

I personally think it's fair to make sure that teenagers fully understand what behavior is expected of them. If they cross the line and break a rule, they should know what the punishment should be. I find that, in the heat of a moment, it's all too easy to tell children they are grounded for life, which, of course, you won't follow through on. By having a list of boundaries and punishments, it takes all the guesswork out.

BABYSITTERS AND NANNIES

It's one thing for *you* to deal with your kids, but what happens when you're not around? There are some children who could even make Mary Poppins fly away.

> *I mean, how can I continue to be the bright, vivacious nanny everyone knows and loves if I have to spend all day with the kids?*
>
> —FRAN DRESCHER

Laurel and Matt were both toddlers when I got a call from my brother. One of his close friends decided she really wanted to work as an au pair (nanny). I knew the girl, Maria, and her family very well and thought it would be a wonderful plan. I was working full-time again and really needed someone who was always around. Maria was kind, smart, and a good driver. It was a dream come true for me.

Pop! Here comes reality. While Maria had spent time around my children before, she never had been in charge of taking care of them. Still, how much trouble could a sweet two- and three-year-old be? Maria soon found out.

It was her first full day, and I waved good-bye as I headed to work. I didn't get any phone calls during the day, so I took that as a good sign. Never in my life did I think she wasn't calling because she couldn't! Less than an hour after I left, Maria had to use the restroom. Being smart parents, when the kids became mobile, we had reversed the door handles so they couldn't accidentally lock themselves in. When Maria went into the room, like most toddlers, they wanted to follow her. Maria wasn't ready for an audience, so she firmly said, "No" and closed the door. Apparently, that wasn't the answer they wanted. When she tried to exit the restroom, the door wouldn't budge. They had locked her in from the outside! To this day I can't believe it was intentional, but . . .

Let me divert to add a restroom follow-up story. After the experience with Matt and Laurel, we decided to keep doorknobs as they were. Then along came Wolf. By two years old, he was clever enough to push a chair to the shelves and pull out a cookie box. He'd take it and sneak off to the bathroom to demolish the entire box in solitude.

One day the babysitter saw him at the tail end of his cookie caper and walked over to the bathroom to look in. The moment he spotted her, he closed the door and locked it. I arrived home from work a few minutes later to a frantic babysitter and a sobbing boy. I didn't know he knew how to operate the lock, which was a latch above the doorknob that you had to turn. Have you ever seen one of those wooden baby lock-and-latch boxes? I bought one because I thought letting him fiddle with it would help his fine motor skills. It did. Unfortunately, he found out it was easier to lock it than unlock it. The hinges were on the inside, so we couldn't take the door off that way. Wolf began to sob. After twenty minutes of talking him through the process, he finally got the door open.

The next day on my TV show, my cohosts and I talked about the incident, and I made an offhanded comment about him learning a lesson. Harmless, right? Not to one viewer, who must have been half listening and didn't understand the full story. She called the children's welfare services division and filed a child abuse complaint!

When the investigator called, he asked if my son had been locked in a bathroom.

I said yes.

He asked why we'd left him in the bathroom, and I explained we couldn't get the door open because the lock and hinges were inside. He actually asked me if I'd considered kicking the door down.

Now, stop and think about that for a moment, and you'll realize why there are so many problems in the child welfare system. Wolf was right in front of the door. If we'd kicked the door down, Wolf would have been seriously injured. I explained the obvious to the investigator, and he let go of that track of thought.

But he kept coming back to the statement, "So you left him locked in a bathroom sobbing for twenty minutes."

Well, yes, we did, but there was really no other option. He finally became convinced that we weren't locking children up intentionally and abusing them and dropped the complaint.

My advice now? No locks on either side of the door.

Back to the babysitter story. What Maria's experience shows is that children can behave far differently when you aren't around. While I won't say it takes a village to raise your child, there are certain people whom you should entrust with some authority, but make sure they are ready for the unexpected.

From G. B. in Vermont:

I am the father of six children. Four were born in the first four years. When you have a large family, cooperation is a must. We keep a chart on the refrigerator with each of the children's names. Every time they disobey, they get a mark on the chart. Each week we tally the marks. They can have three marks with no consequences. For example, if they didn't clean their rooms, they would first be reminded, and then they would get a mark. They would have a certain amount of time to correct the situation, and if they still didn't clean the room, they would get another mark. We also let babysitters mark the chart, which means the kids have to treat them as authority figures too.

One day my son caused trouble on the school bus, so we gave the bus driver an index card, and she'd give it to us if she had any problems! Some parents talk about their children behaving one way with them and a different way when they aren't around. We involved everyone so that they were trained to have good, consistent behavior.

GAME NIGHT OR FIGHT NIGHT?

From D. S. in Wisconsin:

We have two boys that are in their twenties now. The youngest just served two tours in Iraq with the marines, and the older one is married with two kids. They both turned out fine despite their numerous antics while growing up. They only recently shared this story with me.

When they were little, we lived in a small, ranch-style home. We had a lovely babysitter but never had an inkling what happened when we weren't home. The boys told me they would throw their toys up on the roof, which forced the babysitter to get a ladder to retrieve them. When she would get to the top of the ladder, they would begin to shake it. I doubt it was what they intended, but one day the sitter fell off and broke her leg. She never told us why, and we always wondered why she never agreed to baby-sit for us again. After just learning this from my grown boys, I am still stunned that she didn't haul us into court!

> *Your children tell you casually years later what it would have killed you with worry to know at the time.*
>
> —MIGNON MCLAUGHLIN

Have you ever planned a family night and it turned into *fight night*? It sounds corny, but I promise that once you try this a few times, you will see that family night can be something even your older kids will look forward to.

Matt came home one day and said he wanted a game night. We hadn't played a board game for years, and I honestly didn't think the older kids would want to. They did! We played Monopoly for two hours after dinner, and the children made me promise to repeat game night again the next week. It was a wonderful, fun family time. Unfortunately, it doesn't always end up that way.

From D. J. in Tennessee:

This past weekend we were having a family game night. It ended up being a *kids fighting night*. My daughter and son got into an argument. From there it went to them throwing poker chips (we were playing Michigan Rummy) at each other, and it just kept escalating. When I tried to step in, neither of them wanted to listen, and they just kept at it, yelling and throwing.

Now you might think what I did next was a little off, but it worked. I walked out of the room and told both of them that I would be back when they were finished.

My nineteen-year-old followed me, saying, "Mom, are you crazy? They're going to kill each other in there."

I told her to sit back and watch. Sure enough it got worse. But in awhile it got better. When they were both out of chips to throw, they retreated to separate corners in silence. I came back in.

Now you think it might have ended there, but *no*! My daughter wasn't finished yet. When the nineteen-year-old and I came back into the room, we started picking up the chips. Yes, I probably should have forced the other two to help, but why start the fighting all over again? The house was quiet. My daughter was on the couch, and my son was in his room. Blissful silence! Ahhh.

Then it was shattered. The trouble-making daughter got off the couch and loudly insisted that she should get to help pick up the chips. I told her I really didn't want any help, and I would prefer if she would leave the room. That insulted her, and she demanded that I let her clean. I continued telling her that she was not needed and to go upstairs. She finally gave up and started up the stairs but then decided to add some *colorful* comments.

At that point I stated, "You're grounded," but before I could finish my sentence, she laughed and said I couldn't ground her since she had to go to school and to her after-school activities.

To that I replied I wasn't finished. I said, "You are grounded from the Internet for a week. Bring your laptop down to me now." It took a few requests, but eventually her laptop was handed to me.

My son then came in, too, and asked if I needed help. When I said no, he said, "Okay, I'll just go and sit down upstairs." He still had his laptop!

I could go on forever about how effective the removal of privileges is and tell you story after story. My three kids have three very different personalities, and what works for one doesn't necessarily work for the other. I tell them, "The law states that I have to provide you with a roof, utilities, clothes, and food. Anything else is a privilege. The TV, game system, computer, Internet, cell phone, and, yes, even the doors on your room are privileges. Treat them that way."

EMBRACE YOUR ROLE

The moral of this chapter is to embrace your job as a parent. Your children don't need you to be a friend. They need for you to be a parent, mentor, and role model. You can be your child's greatest advocate and supporter, but that doesn't mean you accept everything at face value, and it doesn't mean that you will do anything and everything they ask of you so that they will *like* you. It means loving them enough that you're willing to take on the job of parenting. It's a lifelong commitment.

> *If you have never been hated by*
> *your child, you have never been a parent.*
> —BETTE DAVIS

From D. L. in Florida:

My wife and I have two very well behaved children (at least most of the time). However, we have found that the most important thing is to be consistent with discipline. This is extremely important as I have been serving in Iraq for the last four months, so my wife has to do all the disciplining. We also abide by something my mother used to tell me. She said that you need to give your children your attention when they are good; otherwise, they will try to get it by being bad.

I wholeheartedly concur. You shouldn't focus on your children just when they're doing something wrong that you need to punish. It's just as important to praise them when they do something right.

I won't pretend to have all the answers, but I do know this: the so-called experts don't know any more than what most parents instinctively feel. Your family is unique. What works for another parent may not work for you or your child, but they may offer you some options to try. Don't let anyone spoon-feed you the answers to perfect parenting. They probably don't know any more than you do. If your love for your children and desire to raise them well is what guides your actions, you probably won't go too far off the proper path. Granted, it's an uneven path, there are bramble bushes along the way, and occasionally you'll have to double back to pick up the trail again, but it's the path you have chosen, and you can navigate it successfully.

Before I got married I had six theories about bringing up children; now I have six children, and no theories.

—JOHN WILMOT

Ca-ching, Ca-ching:
The Allowance Lowdown

If you want to recapture your youth, just cut off his allowance.

—AL BERNSTEIN

We had an interesting discussion with our son Collin yesterday. He asked, "If I need a new bike helmet, would you pay for half?"

Joe and I looked at each other, back at him, and then stated the obvious: "You already have a bike helmet, and it's on your head right now."

"I know," came the reply, "but I'm just wondering, if I needed one, whether you'd help me pay for it."

At this point every parent knows his child is angling for something. At this age, children simply don't come around to have philosophical discussions about the theoretical value of bike helmets in the age of automobiles. There was a point, and Collin wasn't getting to it. The conversation continued:

Us: But you don't need a new helmet.
Collin: I know, but what if I did?
Us: But you don't.
Collin: I know. I'm just asking.
Us: Okay. What do you really want?

Collin: Nothing. Honest.

Us: [after a pause to try to quickly analyze what might really be going on] If you *needed* a bike helmet and didn't have one, we would pay the entire price of the helmet because that's a basic safety necessity.

Collin: Oh. [And he exited.]

If you want children to keep their feet on the ground, put some responsibility on their shoulders.

—ABIGAIL VAN BUREN

Flash forward one day. We were leaving on a family bike trip to go geocaching (treasure hunting—it's a wonderful sport our whole family enjoys) along a beach. J. D. put on Joe's helmet. Joe called him back and told him they needed to switch. J. D. said he didn't like the helmet he had, and he was going back inside to get a different one. We looked at each other and figured he'd be back quickly, since there is only one bike helmet per person. To our surprise, he came back wearing a different helmet. Whose? Not Collin's. It was Matt's. Collin was just fronting the questions for Matt, who wanted a fashionable new helmet like Collin's, which he could adorn with stickers. He had Collin approach us to feel out whether we'd help him pay for it. After learning we wouldn't, he bought his own.

We are always leery about conversations like that one because when children desperately want a new version of something they already own, we have noticed a strange coincidence. The object they already have disappears. Gone like the wind. It happened a couple of times with school backpacks before we wised up. A friend showed up with a cooler one at school, and our child wanted it too. Since a backpack is a school necessity, we would have to buy a new one. Now, when we face a similar disappearance that smells fishy, we find a replacement at home. Somehow, after learning they will be using their little sister's Dora the Explorer backpack, their own backpacks mysteriously reappear. Hmmm. Quite curious. Our rule is that we will buy the necessities, and the kids have to use the money they save to buy anything else they want.

To pay for what they desire, they need money. Now, I know we live in a society that celebrates capitalism, but since when did it become a rite of passage in kindergarten to demand an allowance? I think an allowance is a good idea since it allows children to make their own responsible choices about what is important to spend their money on. The idea is if they have to pay for the movie or iTunes, they'll only pay for the ones they really want, instead of begging us for everything.

Golf champion Tiger Woods said, "I'm tight. I mean . . . because I never had a whole lot growing up as a kid . . . I always had to save. Then I'd buy like one big thing, like a pair of basketball shoes or something like that. But I had to save up my allowance." Tiger obviously turned out fine. And it won't ruin my kids either.

GIVEN OR EARNED?

The next question is whether an allowance is something to be *given* or *earned* for performing chores. Most children, of course, think the former is most appropriate. My experience was the latter. When we were growing up, we had weekly chores that we did in exchange for our allowance. Every Saturday my sister and I cleaned our rooms (really my sister cleaned mine too; she was a cleaning nut). We vacuumed and dusted the whole house. We were only allowed to play with our toys in our bedrooms or in the basement, and we had to pick them up as soon as we were finished playing with them. Every evening, from the time we were five years old, we took turns washing and drying the dishes. We both hated to wash, so taking turns was the only fair way. None of these chores were punishment; they were just expected.

Actually, there was a period every summer when I would love washing dishes but only for a couple of weeks. Why? I had just returned from Girl Scout camp. I attended Camp Chippewa Bay in Chippewa Falls, Wisconsin, from nine years of age until I was twelve. We were split up into groups, and each girl was given a different job every few days. The worst job, of course, was latrine duty (we called it *potty patrol*), which meant that you had to clean the toilets by scrubbing them until they were sparkling, and then you had to do the same with the sinks and the floors. Another job was raising and lowering the flag, but I was always so worried that the flag would touch the ground on my watch that I actually dreaded that job. There was also setting the table, serving the food, clearing the food, washing the dishes, and drying the dishes.

It always amazed me that washing the dishes at Camp went so quickly. One girl would clear the plate and hand it to me. I would then wash the plate and hand it to the person who had drying duty. The whole stack of dishes seemed to be done in minutes flat. Why couldn't it just be that way at home? I hit upon the answer; my parents simply didn't have the right system set up. Each year when I came home from camp, I was determined to change it. To start with, I have a bit of a take-charge personality, which was in full evidence at times like these. I would assign my brother to clear the table and scrape the plates. I would wash the plates and hand them to my sister. It wouldn't take too long for me to become frustrated. They simply didn't work quickly enough! I was certain their inadequacies were due to their lack of the exceptional training I had been privileged to receive at Camp Chippewa Bay. I would admonish them to work more diligently and remind them how quickly the job would go if they would only follow my system. Sometimes it took two weeks, and sometimes it took four weeks, but my newfound love of dishwashing diminished nonetheless. Love it or not, I still had to do it.

I recall a traumatic experience in my young life that really helped shape my thoughts about allowances. My parents gave me thirty cents for allowance. Ten cents went to the Sunday school collection basket. Ten cents went to my weekly Girl Scout troop dues collection. And ten cents went to me for my candy collection. It worked out well. Then, one week the troop dues increased to twenty-five cents. Even after shifting over my candy money, I was still unable to cover my debts. I know it sounds silly, but this is how the mind of a third grader works. At least, it's how mine did. I fretted. I thought. I cried. I simply couldn't figure out what to do. I knew that money for God's work doesn't get touched. For some reason I felt uncomfortable mentioning my dilemma to my parents. In my young mind, I figured they must have known what a precarious financial position I was in, since my mother was the troop leader.

I thought, *If she knows the dues went up and she knows I get thirty cents for allowance, she must be sending me a message. I have to quit Girl Scouts.*

I wasn't sure why she'd want to lead a troop without her daughter in it, but I knew what went on in the minds of adults was sometimes confusing. The evening before my next Girl Scout meeting, I finally got the courage to go talk to my parents. Through tears I explained that I had to quit Girl Scouts, and a look of bewilderment crossed their faces. They were baffled. It turned out that they didn't view my finances from a child's perspective and had been totally unaware of my situation. They raised my allowance fifteen cents to cover the dues. My candy money stayed the same. Drat!

Later, when I was in about the sixth grade, I remember having the feeling of owning the world. I had seven dollars saved. I could buy just about anything my heart desired. No amount of Cracker Jack was seemingly out of my reach. I could even extend loans to my brother. I was a financial titan! When you look at money through a child's eyes, it looks vastly different.

Well, I'm the adult now, and I try not to forget the experiences from my younger days. Allowances are a good idea. It helps children understand the basics of money management. It empowers them to a limited extent. But allowances have changed. Now it seems kids are in the driver's seat. They demand the money they're *due*. Frequently, they don't even have to do anything for it. Granted, there are limited things you want a seven-year-old responsible for doing, but he should do *something*. I didn't start giving allowances until the kids were in the third grade. I figured they really didn't need money for anything. We lived too far from town for them to walk to the candy store, and anything they really needed we would buy for them anyway. But something happened that caused me to have a change of heart.

FLEECING YOUR FRIENDS?

One of our middle sons, J. D., really liked GI Joes. In fact, he liked anything military. To this day his favorite books are about military history. On school holidays he would come to work with me. There was a Dollar General Store just down the block, and it was his favorite place to stop and shop. If you've never been to one of these types of stores, you've really missed an experience. Everything is one dollar or very close to it. You'll find soap, underwear, knives, toys, books, crystal lamps. I never saw a dining room table in there, but I may have missed it. So on these vacation days, I'd take him over there and let him pick out a couple of items. Usually he'd select an army truck, a chopper, and a figurine. Over a number of trips, he built up a fighting force most countries would envy.

A few months later, I walked into his room, and he was showing one of his older brothers a wad of cash. I was stunned. Where did it come from? He gave me that shrug that's been perfected by children and Frenchmen. Shoulders and eyebrows arched upward, sides of the mouth down, blank look in the eye. You know the gesture. When forced to put forth a verbal answer, I got, "I dunno." And finally, "I saved it." Saved it? How? He didn't get an allowance. It turned out that my son with the angelic eyes and cute grin was a cunning and cutthroat businessman.

He would take a couple of the toys to school to play with on the bus at the end of the day. The other boys would see them and also thought they were cool. J. D. would explain that he had only a couple, but for a certain price he might be willing to part with one. No one apparently caught on to the fact that each time he sold a tank or a truck or an army lieutenant, there would be another to replace it fairly soon. Here is the craziest part of it all: the price. While I was buying one-dollar toys, he was flipping them for twenty dollars! Yep, that was my reaction too. First, who would pay that for a cheap bit of plastic, and second, what third grader had that kind of money? Now that I think about it, maybe they were all running their own after-school businesses!

To make matters worse, one of his best customers was also one of his best friends. I won't name him because we are good friends with his parents, and I'm embarrassed about the whole business set-up to this day. This boy was given a very large allowance. Money in the hands of a small boy with an equally small level of experience in purchasing items and an even smaller cognizance of the value of a dollar is an unwise and costly combination. Whereas J. D. grasped the economics of the perceived scarcity-of-products business model and had been operating this homegrown enterprise for months and had several hundred dollars.

So as a parent, what do you do? Congratulate him for recognizing the price the market was willing to pay for a commodity and for hyping the small supply to increase the demand? Or do you berate him for taking advantage of friends? I decided to do both since, after all, he had already told me he wanted to work in the business world as an adult. I explained that it's wrong to take advantage of a friend. He argued back that his friend had no qualm paying the asking price. Point to J. D. Next, I decided to play to his clearly clever business acumen. I said that when his friend realized he had overpaid for an item, then he would be hesitant to buy anything from J. D. in the future. The effect would be that J. D.'s client list would dry up. The long-term business impact would be negative. That hit home. Megapoint to Mom.

ALLOWING FOR ALLOWANCES

After that event, I decided it might be time for an allowance for all the big kids. I talked to some friends and came to the conclusion that a dollar for each year of their age was about right. I discussed it with the kids, and they seemed to think it was fair. I explained that the money would not just be given to them; they were getting it in exchange for chores they would need to perform. That's where I made a fatal error. I didn't specify exactly what chores each specific child had to do.

> *People forget how fast you did a job,*
> *but they remember how well you did it.*
>
> —HOWARD NEWTON

I'd say, "Laurel, you need to help with the kitchen chores and caring for the little kids," and "J. D., you need to tidy your room and take clothes down to the laundry room." Now, put yourself in a kid's position—a lazy kid's position.

Laurel thought kitchen chores meant turning on the dishwasher after someone else had rinsed the plates, loaded the dishwasher, and added the soap. To her credit she is great at helping to look after the younger kids.

J. D., like most young boys, earnestly believes that any room where you can't *see* anything lying about is a tidy room. That means putting yesterday morning's cereal bowl (which he wasn't supposed to have in his room anyway) inside the bathroom closet until green dots are growing on it is well within the norms of cleanliness. Every item of dirty clothing would be stuffed under the bed or way to the back of the drawers. When he was feeling particularly economical, he'd simply wear the same shirt for days in a row. Following a young boy's line of reasoning, only clothes in the clothes hamper qualify as items that need to be taken to the laundry room. So if you wore clothes for a long time, then stuffed them out of sight, you could conceivably make your trips to the laundry room as scarce as harmony on family Christmas card photo day. Within a very short period of time, you could smell him before he entered the room.

Business guru Peter Drucker said, "Plans are only good intentions unless they immediately degenerate into hard work." That's not how the children viewed it: they knew they had chores, and they knew they'd get around to them eventually. Since they *intended* to do it, they figured everything was okay. They also thought I was so busy that I wouldn't check on whether they were actually doing their chores or not. There are so many people moving around our house at any given time that someone was bound to pick up the slack. Further, they were ticked off because I would either forget to give them their allowances on time, or if I remembered the allowances, I seemed to have forgotten to go to the ATM and was out of cash. They became convinced this was a slave-labor ploy I had cooked up to keep them in servitude. They were ready to picket. And I was ready to pull my hair out.

WOOF, MEOW, TWITCH, SILENCE

The biggest chore at our house is taking care of the pets. At the moment we only have one dog, Duffy, from the Adopt-a-Dog animal shelter; a farm cat the kids named Snowball, despite the fact that she's dark gray; a rabbit named Bunny Foo Foo; a hedgehog—like every other hedgehog in America—named Spike; and a fish tank. I'd say we have fish and tell you their names, except for the inconvenient fact that despite diligently buying a couple of small fish every two weeks, they simply disappear. Where? Jacques Cousteau said, "The best way to understand fish is to become a fish." Unfortunately, my scuba tank doesn't fit in the three-inch-wide Picture-Frame Fish Tank that my husband bought on one of his way-too-frequent, long-haul flights. Something eerie happens on trips over six hours—a strange biological phenomenon occurs; the brain simply stops thinking rationally, leading a person to believe he desperately needs and will actually use the items in *SkyMall* magazine.

> *Did you ever walk into a room and forget why you walked in? I think that's how dogs spend their lives.*
>
> —SUE MURPHY

At first, we suspected the Beta fish ate the others until it, too, went missing. Could they all be hiding out in the underwater pirate ship? No, there was nothing there or in the treasure chest. Let me get a bit off story line here and ask something: who comes up with the items pet stores sell for fish tanks? My guess is someone obsessed with Johnny Depp's *Pirates of the Caribbean* movies. All sunken ships for sale are pirate ships. Just try to find a toppled schooner or Quint's fishing boat, *Orca*, with shark-bite marks and the back half missing. They're nowhere to be found. And what's up with the treasure chests? Keeping in mind that fish are color-blind, who came up with the idea of styling them with flourescent colors applied with all the precision of a five-year-old let loose with a Spinmaster paint toy? And what kind of pet is a fish anyway? They don't make any sound. You have no idea whether they care one iota about your existence; in fact, they would probably prefer you take your pirate vessel and disappear.

> *Humans are the only animals that have children on purpose*
> *with the exception of guppies, who like to eat theirs.*
>
> —P. J. O'ROURKE

Anyway, back to the missing fish. I thought they might have gone up the aerator tube but realized it was too small. It remains an unsolved mystery, and we keep adding fish to our Bermuda Triangle fish tank. There is one possible explanation offered up by a couple we met at the Boathouse Restaurant in Lakeville, Connecticut, one night. They had taken their four-year-old daughter to the movie theater to see *Finding Nemo*. They knew she would like it because she loved watching the fish in their tank at home. The morning after the movie, they woke up to find the fish gone. They, too, were doing the same pirate-ship-treasure-box search that we had done when their daughter came in and said, "All drains lead to the ocean." It's a famous line from the movie and describes how Nemo makes his escape from the dentist's office so he can return to the ocean. Their daughter had flushed the fish. I viewed our children through squinted eyes as they vigorously shook their heads in denial.

Our hedgehog is another pet I don't understand. I assume the term *pet* comes from what you normally do to an animal that you domesticate. But try petting Spike. I think of Spike as one of the high school kids with the tight-fitting black jeans, Ramones T-shirts, a cigarette pack outlined in his back pocket, gravity defying black-blue hair, and a studded leather wrist strap. You know the kid I'm describing. That's Spike.

Thinking that Spike might enjoy some companionship, we decided—since we had been able to successfully combine two very different families and live together in relatively peaceful harmony—perhaps, we could perform the same socialization magic with Spike and . . . Bunny Foo Foo. Think of Bunny Foo Foo as the nice-but-dumb girl in school. She knows she's not going to outwit anyone, so she relies on your liking her. Bunnies are like that with their big, round, innocent eyes; their fluffiness; and the cute little hop they do. If they sit there, twitch, and look adorable, they figure you'll have to like them. We started with two cages, one for each, and moved them next to each other. I don't know how—or even if—the various species in the animal kingdom communicate, but I figured that making them neighbors was the best first step before having them room together. I feel sorry for them sitting in their cages alone. Yes, they get to play with the kids—well, Spike doesn't really play; he just uncurls and grabs at the worms the kids have—but it seems that playing with other animals simply must be more fun for them.

You should see the cat and dog. After the initial hair-raised, arched back from Snowball and the front paws stretched out on the ground, butt in the air, tail wagging so fast it could double as a flyswatter greeting from Duffy, the two got along. Actually they kind of play this game, and if you have a cat, you've probably seen it before. The cat really wants to play with the dog but feels it would be degrading to actually have to show it, so she simply walks by and pauses to give the dog time to run up. If the dog doesn't catch on, she comes and sits in front of him to preen. Finally, the dog gets it. Hey, maybe she wants to play . . . duh. The dog does a little run forward, stops, and waits for a response. At this point the cat is tired of playing hard to get and runs. The dog takes off in hot pursuit. And the chase is on. When the cat is tired of running, she stops, and if the dog doesn't get the picture that the game is over, she swats him . . . claws out. Anyway, they could get along, so why couldn't Spike and Bunny Foo Foo? At least that's the track my train of thought was chugging along on.

After a week of adjustment, I let Spike and Bunny Foo Foo have some playtime outside the cages. I let them run around the garage. The family that plays together stays together, right? It seemed to work fine. Spike can actually move pretty quickly once he's out in the open, and Bunny Foo Foo loves to hop. They could exercise together! After the excursion we moved them into the nice, big new cage together. I watched them a bit. I made sure each was put in front of his/her own water bottle and food bowl. All seemed fine, so I went inside. Less than ten minutes later I heard a commotion. Bunny Foo Foo had invaded Spike's personal space a bit too quickly. Spike let her know it. Bunny Foo Foo's nose wasn't bleeding, but it was obvious Spike had given her a little jab. Okay, enough with the social experiment. It would be incumbent on the kids to play with them.

I was surprised when I went to the pet store and inquired about the best way for children to exercise a hedgehog and a rabbit. They have leashes! Yes, just like dogs. I bought one for each and went home to let the children get to work with the critters. I helped the kids harness them and get them to the backyard, and then I went inside. In less than five minutes there was pandemonium. The pet harness is one of those inventions that's good in theory but not in its actual utilization.

Bunny Foo Foo had wiggled out of the contraption in no time flat and was enjoying freedom. She hopped here and hopped there and hopped just about everywhere except close enough to the kids so they could catch her. This is where a mother's mind is invaluable. We know how to get anything and anyone's attention—food. Out came the big, orange, lovely carrot sticks. What bunny could resist them? Not Bunny Foo Foo. The kids looked at me as if I'd invented the light switch. Spike, too, quickly outsmarted the fabric-and-Velcro combination that had seemed like such a brilliant design. Fortunately, he isn't able to run fast enough to even outpace the three-year-old. Still, he got a good workout, but you have to watch him every second. We decided having the kids exercise the pets in the garage was the safest solution for everyone.

So far, we have escaped getting the kids a bird. What kind of pet is that? You can't take birds to the park. You can't play with them. They are easily fooled into thinking a mirror is actually a friend, which leads them to, in essence, spend all their time focused on themselves. In fact, they seem to dislike being people pets so much that you have to clip their wings to keep them from escaping. Also, what other pet could you trick into sleeping just by putting a towel over its cage?

As I mentioned, taking care of the pets is the biggest chore at our house. J.D. was *supposed* to be taking care of the critters each morning before school. Did you notice the emphasis on *supposed*? It was intentional. I realized what was going on, or not, when the cat started relying on the local field mice population for sustenance while the dog began eyeing the cat and drooling with desire. What was lacking was a very specific chore list that no one could claim to misunderstand.

ONLINE ALLOWANCES

One of our business correspondents at the television station, who doesn't even have kids, mentioned an interesting allowance concept based on debit cards and Web sites. It's basically a debit card for teens. I chose to go with the one at payjr.com. I was able to set up all inclusive Web pages. The cut-off age for a debit card is twelve, but for the younger kids, you can set up an allowance chart. It's just like the ones we used to pin up on the refrigerator, except kids forget to look at the refrigerator in their rush to grab a drink and run off so quickly the refrigerator door doesn't have time to shut. Anyway, you can select a chore from a list they have or create your own list. You also select the amount paid for each chore and whether you need to verify it's been done or not before being instructed to pay for it.

> *A human being must have occupation if he*
> *or she is not to become a nuisance to the world.*
>
> —DOROTHY L. SAYERS

J. D. is now responsible for watering the houseplants, feeding the dog, cat, rabbit, fish, and hedgehog each day, and making his bed before leaving for the school bus. After he completes the chores, he goes online to his own page on the Web site and checks off the chores he has completed. Since I remember how wily he was with the earlier army-tank side business, I make sure that I verify the chores and have to add my own checkmark. After that is done, I am automatically sent an e-mail at the end of each week, letting me know that it's allowance time and exactly what I owe him. This works well because while I even forget to look at what's on the refrigerator door, I never forget to look at my e-mails. Ah, the modern life.

The older kids are given a debit card. The concept is the same: you select the chores, the price, and the frequency. Each day they are e-mailed a reminder of the chores they need to do and can check them off. Here's the twist: once I verify that the chores have been done, the Web site will auto-matically arrange a transfer from my checking account to their payjr.com debit card. This works very well. When the children want to earn extra money, they can choose from a number of additional chores I've listed that need to be done. Because the credit card companies realize how clever children are, they make it impossible for the kids to get to any of the financial setup pages. That way they can't arrange to pay themselves twenty dollars for brushing their teeth. They also can't get to any siblings' pages to mess with them. Each child has his own login name and password that takes him to his page only.

This summer it's worked even better. While Matt was at summer camp and not doing chores, I agreed to still give him some money since he now had to buy his own shampoo, toothpaste, and the like. I could automatically transfer it onto the card without fiddling with sending a check to him and his having to find a place to cash it. The only downside is that the transfer of funds costs fifty cents; so if the allowance is only three dollars, that can get pricey, comparatively speaking. In that case you can request that the transfer go through only when the level owed reaches a certain amount. I set it at thirty dollars. That means once the payment for chores completed reaches that level, the transfer will go through.

Here are three of the Web sites that offer these types of services. I'm sure you can find more, and I don't recommend one over the other:

pocketcard.com

allowcard.com

upsidevisa.com

> *Work saves us from the three great evils: boredom, vice, and need.*
>
> —VOLTAIRE

CHART OF CHORES

Nothing builds character better than daily and weekly chores. Chores should vary by age and skill.

Here is a basic setup:

Ages 15–17:
- Help the littler ones get dressed while I make breakfast
- Watch the youngest children while I'm making dinner
- Thoroughly clean their own bedrooms and bathrooms
- Do their own laundry

Ages 13–14:
- Clean pets' cages weekly
- Take out trash
- Help with larger projects around house

Ages 11–12:
- Fill the pets' water jugs and feed them morning and night
- Sweep the kitchen floor after every meal
- Wash kitchen, mudroom, and bathroom floors on Saturday
- Clean bathroom toilet weekly
- Clean bathroom tub, mirrors, sink, counter, and faucet
- Fill water jugs for plants as needed
- Help fold and sort laundry
- Make their beds daily

Ages 9–10:
- Vacuum bedrooms and stairs weekly; revacuum if necessary.
- Dry the floors after they have been washed
- Clean kitchen sink, counter, and faucet twice a week
- Make their beds
- Get plates, silverware, cups, and napkins for meals
- Help with loading and unloading dishwasher

Ages 7–8:

- Get food from pantry to restock kitchen
- Help sweep
- Help fold and sort clothes
- Make their beds
- Clean mirrors in main-floor bathroom twice a week
- Sweep mudroom and main-floor bath twice a week
- Help younger children

Age 5-6:

- Take dirty clothes to laundry room
- Sort laundry into red/blue and light colors to wash
- Empty dishwasher—stack plates, bowls, and silverware onto counter, load dishwasher periodically during day and after meals
- Clean certain windows and glass doors twice a week

Toddlers:

- Get dressed—two changes of clothes *maximum* per day (not ten!)
- Keep toys and movies picked up in living room
- Straighten shoes at back door in morning and at night
- Run errands with Mommy
- Get clean diaper, take wrapped one to trash
- General toy pickup throughout house every evening

All children:

- Carry dirty dishes to sink, rinse if able

OFF TO WORK I GO

My eldest child just reached working age . . . almost. I still had to fill out a parental consent form for someone to be able to employ her, and she could only work specific hours. Over the summer I was kind of surprised by the reaction I sometimes got when people would ask me what the kids were doing for the summer. When I mentioned Laurel's job, where she worked, and what she did, some people seemed surprised.

> *Life grants nothing to us mortals without hard work.*
>
> —HORACE

Here's the little secret. Do you wonder why kids don't have a great work ethic? Ever wonder why the president of the United States says illegal immigrants take the jobs Americans don't want? It's because a lot of people raise their children to think they're too good for certain jobs. I'm not saying you should tell your child to aspire to be a dishwasher or a stock boy, but it's certainly a fine way at a young age to learn about the value of money and diligent labor.

To be truthful, Laurel initially said there were only certain jobs she'd take. She wanted to work at one of the trendy Main Street stores in the town we were living. Why? So she could get the discount on clothing at the store. Let's start with the fact that even with the discount she couldn't afford the clothing, and I certainly wouldn't buy it. It was really the attitude of picking and choosing at fifteen that bugged me. I mentioned getting a job at the grocery store as I did at her age, and she blew a gasket. What would her friends think? No one else she knew was working there. The insinuation was that it was beneath her. There's a quick fix for that. I told her, "There are only two places I'll let you work: the grocery store in town or (where I knew my friends, John and Robin, would help her understand the value of hard work) the country store up the road." Hello, Round Hill Country Store!

Anyway, it was the last week of school, and as in many schools the days were filled with class parties, assemblies, and such. The kids really hadn't had much, if any, actual class work, so many of the older kids made evening plans. Wednesday night, they went to the movies; Thursday night was pizza and youth group, which is normally the only night out during the week for my kids; Friday was the last day of the school year, so there was a class party in the afternoon at one of the children's homes. That evening, another child's family threw a party with parents invited.

Saturday, I assumed my fifteen-year-old daughter, Laurel, would begin her summer job of cleaning, making coffee, and doing all the odd jobs at the nearby country store. Instead, she didn't wake up until eleven o'clock, and even then she was grumpy. You know how they come into the kitchen with that semiscowl on their faces, hair disheveled, dragging their feet? The attitude is, "Yeah, I stayed up too late, but my bad mood is really your fault."

I knew her shift at the store was supposed to be 6:00 A.M. until noon, but I figured maybe on the first day after school, they were having her work a different shift. Nope. When I asked if her shift was starting late, she snapped back in that surly, tired-teen way that she is a person, too, and needs fun in her life, so she had taken the week off and would start work next week. Wait, she'd been running around with friends for the past three nights, hadn't she? That didn't count. In teenage time, school during the day cancels out the fun in the evening. She was starting from scratch. I reminded her that she needed to earn all of her spending money for the next school year when she would be away from home, there was a limited number of weeks during the summer, and that hanging out with friends wasn't making her any wealthier.

I explained to Laurel that as you mature and become old enough for a job, you take on more responsibility. In this case, she needed help realizing what her goal should be. Few kids have any real concept of money. They go to dinner and a movie, and Mom or Dad pays. They want a cool shirt, and Mom or Dad often buys it. Laurel needed me to help her understand the meaning of money, especially now that it was going to be her money. Time for Math 101.

Ten months of school means forty weekends. A movie on one night, plus popcorn and a drink, is $20. That means $800 just to cover movies for the school year. What? Yikes! Yes, $800 if you want to go to a movie with friends each weekend. Frankly, that would be a cheap Saturday night. If she wants to go to Six Flags Over Texas, she needs $42 just for the ticket. That means working one day (6 hours at $7.65 an hour) will just barely cover the ticket, and oh, by the way, the $7.65 is *before* taxes. Yes, the first paycheck did lead to an interesting conversation about why the government needs so much of the money she earns.

At the beginning of the summer, I really wasn't sure what kind of work ethic would come through. To my delight, after her slow start, she worked as much as possible and, in fact, took on more jobs, including helping out at my friend Rebecca's restaurant, working for a catering company, and babysitting often for one of my coworkers. Now that school has begun, we'll see if she blows it all right away or is able to control her spending.

From M. C. in Texas:

My three kids are ages fourteen to nineteen. I give them $5 a day for lunch and then $15 more for the week. The kids can do as they like with the lunch money: save it or spend it. My daughter doesn't eat lunch at school. Instead, she keeps the money and stops at Subway after school and then saves the rest. My boys are pretty big strapping guys. The $5 is quickly used up at the lunch bar. But if they want money for Friday night, they make their own lunch at home and save it up for the weekend. If they want to make extra money, I always offer to let them do extra chores. So far this system has worked well and has not been too costly. One boy just got out of high school. Maybe he'll even start earning his own keep soon!

THE BOTTOM LINE

You may be a financial whiz, able to balance a checkbook in seconds flat, and save money for a rainy day with ease. If so, you are unlike most Americans. For the first time since the Great Depression, Americans are spending more than they earn. They aren't just living paycheck to paycheck; they are living beyond their checks. Where is the money going? Frequently to unnecessary items, such as cable TV, expensive cars, the latest fashions, designer sneakers, more meals outside the home.

Financial role modeling is a rare commodity. Today we were at a small-town diner that had a cobweb-filled store attached to it. It appeared as though they had organized a town-wide garage sale and simply kept it in a permanent building all year. While waiting for the food, I took a look around. I found an old mahogany chair with a needlepoint seat. It was lovely and small enough that it would be perfect for an old desk I have but for which I hadn't been able to find a chair. It was thirty-five dollars, and we bought it.

Matt looked at me and said, "You didn't let us buy little bottles of pear juice yesterday at lunch, but in a second today, you decide to buy an old chair. It doesn't make sense."

Yesterday, he wanted to buy a three-ounce bottle of pear juice. It cost three dollars, and he'd have needed to buy about three of them to quench his thirst. I told him he was free to spend his own money if he wanted, but I thought it was ridiculously expensive, and I wouldn't purchase it for him. Not surprisingly, he decided water was just fine. I explained that five of those tiny bottles equaled the cost of a beautiful, antique chair that I really needed. Further, the chair would not only retain its value but would possibly even increase in value over time; therefore, purchasing the chair made financial sense, but purchasing the fancy drinks was akin to throwing away money.

Few people can understand smart money management and the value of work unless they are given lessons. That certainly includes our children. Non-permissive parents understand that not buying their children everything they want and teaching children to work for their money is the loving way to raise responsible children.

*I'm a great believer in luck, and I find
the harder I work the more I have of it.*

—THOMAS JEFFERSON

Fair or Foul: Sportsmanship

It is curious that physical courage should be so common in the world and moral courage so rare.

—MARK TWAIN

Kobe Bryant's basketball team, the LA Lakers, was playing the Dallas Mavericks early in the 2005–2006 season. The game was a foregone conclusion fairly early on. Bryant scored 62 points in the first three quarters and had the chance to contend for the franchise record. Coach Phil Jackson pulled him from the game, saying, "It's a 30-point game." When asked why he did it, Coach Jackson responded, "That's not the spirit of the game." Coach Jackson wanted to win but saw no need to destroy another team in the process.

In contrast, Epiphanny Prince's team, Murray Bergtraum High School, was playing Brandeis High School. The score was 44 to 6 with Bergtraum leading after the first quarter, and the spread widened to 74 to 11 by halftime. Bergtraum High was rated number two in the nation, and Prince was acknowledged to be one of the best players in the nation, evidenced by the scholarship she had already accepted from Rutgers. Prince's team was playing a team they'd beaten earlier that season by running up a 93-point lead.

Prince had the chance to set the record for most points scored in a girls' high school game. Her coach, Ed Grezinsky, faced the same choice Coach Jackson had—deciding whether setting records in an unbalanced game was more important than teaching good sportsmanship. Grezinsky chose the record, telling the *New York Post*, "We thought she had a chance to break the record, so we just let her go." I'm not sure who the *we* was in his statement, but by that time he was taking so much heat that he may have been trying to spread the decision around. Prince scored 113 points in that game and took the record.

The opposing coach, Vera Springer, summed it up this way: "This was an adult decision. Why would you do this against a team like ours? She didn't earn this. It was like picking on a handicapped person."

If you had been the Bergtraum High School coach, which path you would have taken? Clearly, I think that the lack of class and sportsmanship shown by the Murray Bergtraum coach was disgraceful. What life lessons was he teaching these young girls? It was that winning isn't enough if you have the chance to demolish and demoralize others in the process. Coaches should urge their teams to win, but they should pay close attention to the other lessons they are teaching along the way. As Knute Rockne once said, "One man practicing sportsmanship is better than a hundred teaching it."

One of my children attends Greenwich County Day School. Like Coach Jackson, his basketball coach understands the big picture. Near the end of the game this week, the team was winning by enough points that it was unlikely they would lose. As my son relates it, Coach Ledee told the boys that until the end of the game, he wanted them to focus on their passing as much as possible instead of on scoring. There were several lessons. The boys weren't told to stop trying but rather to continue working on areas other than scoring. In doing so, they learned a memorable lesson about winning with class.

THE REAL WINNER

I doubt you've ever heard the following story. In fact, I tried to present it on television because I'd never heard anything like it, but the boy involved refused, saying to me that he didn't want any attention for doing what was right. I left it at that. I can't recall the exact town or the boy's name, but it occurred around 2004.

The setting was the state championship high school football game. The stands were filled, and like all great games, it was a nail-biter to the very end. The score kept changing with the lead going back and forth between the two teams.

As the minutes and seconds ticked down, one team had the lead, but the other team had the ball. The boy ran long, stopped at the three-yard line, and turned to catch the spiral. It was just out of his reach, so he dove for it. Ball and boy came together in the end zone. Or did they? The referee threw his arms up. Touchdown! The boy's team was the state champion. The crowd went wild, erupting into a mixture of cheers from the boy's team's fans, realizing they were victors, and groans from the opposing side, who had come so close.

Suddenly the boy jumped up holding the ball and ran over to the referee. The ref's arms came down, and the crowd became silent. The boy told the referee that the ball had hit the ground before he caught it, and it bounced into his hands. Because his body was blocking the referee's view, it had appeared he caught the ball. The referee reversed his ruling, and the boy's team lost.

I read the weekend recap of the game online in a small newspaper, and I called the boy. It was a powerful story of a young man instantaneously making the right choice when it would have been so easy to have done the opposite. When you're a teenage football player, the state championship is the holy grail. His team could have taken the game, and he would have been hailed a hero for scoring the winning touchdown. No one else knew the ball touched the turf before it touched his hands. But he knew, and he knew it was not the sportsmanlike way to win despite how desperately he wanted his team to take the championship.

I told him I thought his story was powerful and that I wanted the country to see him, meet him, and learn what a great kid he was. He wanted none of it. He told me he simply did the right thing and told the truth. He didn't expect or want any attention. I wished him well and told him his parents had raised a wonderful son. Then I hung up.

I sat stunned by his refusal to accept any accolades. Epiphanny Prince and her team welcomed the spotlight after behavior that many viewed as the antithesis of good sportsmanship. This boy shunned the spotlight he deserved. Even in the loss, the boy, his coach, and his team were the real winners. I wondered what his parents said when he got home, and I wondered what Prince's parents said.

WHAT'S HAPPENED TO SPORTSMANSHIP?

What's happened to sportsmanship? It was ruined by the theory that drives permissive parenting. If you accept that a child will have good self-esteem only if you tell him he is a winner or the best all the time, you have to remove the possibility that he might lose. That's what has occurred.

> *Sportsmanship. Try it.*
>
> —GUARD ENGLEHEART

Do you remember playing sports in kindergarten? They were insignificant games, but there was definitely a winner and a loser. Not today. Why don't more kids think sportsmanship, fair play, and the *game* of the game are what matters most? Why is the behavior of that honest high school football player so rare?

I have a politically incorrect theory (I know, you're shocked) about why kids hold little regard for the traditional idea of fair play. Some intelligent, possibly well-intended researcher decided that games which are won or lost fair and square are judgmental. (I have a feeling that person was likely not the best athlete.) Unlike when I was growing up, many children today aren't allowed to win or lose during their most formative years. Permissive parents compound the problem because their children must be told they are perfect. They played *great* in every game even if they didn't. They are winners, no matter what. Children are taught that rules don't matter. Kicking a goal or making a basket often earns *both* teams a point (remember, since no one can win or lose, that means they have to tie). So later on it could seem very logical that when a coach in high school tells them to cheat, they see that as ethically permissible.

Many youth associations run by parents are in lockstep. A Wisconsin youth baseball association has a page-long list of rules. The rules vary by age group but are strictly observed. They have to do with things such as the number of pitches allowed for Coach Pitch, how many runs can be scored in an inning, and how many batters get to bat in a T-Ball inning. And there's the rule that at the end of each game the teams must be tied.

Then comes the big tournament at the end of the season. No more Mr. Nice Guy! It's cutthroat. All of a sudden every point counts. *What?* Yes, that's what the kids are thinking. After all, they only have experience with tied games. *Why does it matter if I make it to home base before I'm called out? You mean that doesn't also score a run? You mean we can lose?* That's what is going through their minds. As a result, kids end up in tears, and parents aren't far behind them. It further solidifies their theory that it's cruel and unusual punishment for a child or team to lose.

> *It is better to aim at perfection and miss*
> *than to aim at imperfection and hit it.*
> —THOMAS WATSON

Don't get me wrong. I urge my kids to be as competitive as possible and always try to win. But they lose sometimes. That's life. Get used to it. It doesn't change the value of the children in any way. They are still great kids, but they may not be great golfers. One of our eight, I suspect, will be much better at shot put than ice dancing. So what? The real value in sports, other than the enjoyment of the game, is to learn how to lose. That concept is a shock to children raised by permissive parents.

These are children who haven't been prepared for even the slightest adversity. Because they never lose, their parents start to believe it's true and get upset when they are confronted with the fact that their child isn't perfect. But face the facts: no one is perfect, and no one is even great right off the bat. Even Tiger Woods, who was great at a very young age, didn't start out that way. He had to practice. He lost games. His father didn't tell him not to keep score. His dad told him to practice. Smart dad! By the way, it's well documented how much Tiger loved and respected his father. Tiger didn't become great because his dad never allowed him to lose. He's great because he knows how to keep pursuing his goals after he loses.

Today we are led to believe that children's self-esteem will be irreparably harmed if they fail in anything. They won't be able to handle it. The truth is that, from the age of four or maybe even three, kids know the real score, and nothing a parent or coach tells them can change that. Instead, it confuses children. The message is, "You must always win." What about just having fun playing the game? Well, that's terrific, but in the end you always have to *win*.

Which of these two following views about sportsmanship teaches a better life lesson?

1. "When you are playing for the national championship, it's not a matter of life or death. It's more important than that." —Coach Duffy Daugherty, Michigan State
2. "What counts in sports is not the victory, but the magnificence of the struggle." —Coach Joe Paterno, Penn State

Obviously, Coach Paterno is teaching athletes the lessons that will help them as adults. While it's always tantalizing to think that your child might be so good at a sport that it will become his career (and who has a son who doesn't want to become an NFL, NBA, or NHL player?), the reality is much different.

Here are the facts: there are about 37,000 high schools in the United States. That's about 440,000 high school basketball players. Of that number, only about 8,000 make it to college teams. Of that group, only 550 play in the NBA, and only 30 to 40 new players make it to the league each year. Half of those are from outside the United States. *Bottom line:* of the 440,000 high school players in America, less than .005 percent will make it to the NBA. It's unlikely your child, even if he or she is the star of the team, will play pro sports. That means the best thing you can hope for is to have a coach that will teach the team more than just sports. The most valuable lesson isn't how to win but how to lose and keep going.

SPORTS REALITY CHECK

Frightening things must occur when child development experts gather in a room together. Common sense sets off sensors at the door. "*Beep. Beep. Beep. This one will give you problems. He might very well disagree with your fore-gone conclusions . . . Beep. Beep. Beep.* Activating ejection seat."

> *Success is how high you bounce when you hit bottom.*
>
> —GENERAL GEORGE PATTON

Like-minded individuals make the gathering so much nicer and easier. I doubt the always-tie-because-then-everyone-is-a-winner crowd ever played many sports because their theory misses one of the most important aspects of sport: games are not about making people think they are all equal. They are not about making players just as excited about losing as they are about winning. Those are pie-in-the-sky ideas, which even the youngest child can spot as being loony.

We play games to establish teamwork, develop leadership skills, and to teach sportsmanship by learning to accept victory or defeat and keep on try-ing. Somehow, though, the we're-all-winners-every-time experts got schools, sports leagues, and parents to buy into their theories. From the moment many kids are involved in group sports until they hit junior high, their teams tie, which means they don't lose. I've seen sixth-grade teams play football games where there is no score. Even though one side made more touchdowns, the kids are told it was a tie. *What? No it wasn't. That's not fair.* That is the reality of what the kids are thinking.

Instead of teaching them about morals, ethics, perseverance, and grace, the game teaches them they won't be allowed to lose, and the rules don't matter. Sportsmanship means winning fair and square and losing with dignity. It compels players to learn to practice, deal with defeat, and that a winner in life is a person who rises each time he falls. These are real life lessons.

QUITTERS NEVER WIN

We all want our kids to be winners, but it is vastly more important for them to learn that losing doesn't mean the end of the world. They will lose at things all their lives, and they had better get used to it. That doesn't mean they should *enjoy* losing. It means they need to learn they will survive, and if they practice more, they may change the outcome the next time they compete.

> *Adversity causes some men to break; others to break records.*
> —WILLIAM ARTHUR WARD

Sports offer one of the best ways to teach perseverance. A child who learns that lesson early will be a much happier adult. Laurel is on the field hockey team at the Hockaday School, which is known for having some of the best athletic teams in the five-state region. Yesterday, I answered the phone to hear Laurel sobbing on the other end.

"I can't do it. It's too tough. I'm not as good as the other girls. I want to quit," she cried.

I told her she wasn't allowed to quit. She'd made a commitment, and that was that. Sure, I could have told her she was the best player, but she's not. Instead, I told her that she could have practiced more before the season. She missed preseason training, but the coach had given her the daily workout sheet to follow at home. Instead, she chose to do her own workouts, which may not have focused on the strengths she needed for field hockey. I explained that she might need to practice now on weekends.

Her previous coach thought she should lose a few pounds so that she would be more agile. While she isn't overweight, it certainly would help her speed. She was still the same weight.

I explained that no one could make her happy on the team. No one can make her feel that she is a good player. If she practices more and gets in better physical shape, she will likely play better. Then she will know her own actions have taken her to a better place. That's what will give her self-esteem. That's what will make her happy. Knowing she did it herself. Teens are always asking for more control in their lives. Explain that in the big picture that doesn't mean setting their own curfews or picking their own clothes; it means taking control of the decisions that bring them lifelong happiness, self-confidence, and self-esteem. Those can't be given to children; they have to earn them on their own. As I edit this chapter, the season is now over. Guess what? She lost a few pounds, practiced like crazy, and was a starter on the team by the end of the season.

FIXING THE GAME

Too many parents try to *make* their children happy by basically fixing the games. Then the kids hit junior high and high school. All of a sudden the rules that were ignored earlier matter. Why now? Kids are confused. They are told as children that rules don't matter, that kicking a soccer goal earns both teams a point because they have to tie and because anything is fair so long as it keeps someone from losing. Now the rules count, and the officials keep score. The children aren't prepared for it, and that leads to problems.

> *A gold medal is a wonderful thing. But if you're not enough without it, you'll never be enough with it.*
>
> —Cool Runnings

The National Association of Sports Officials keeps track of some of the worst sports behavior:

- In Maryland, a junior high school student smashed his helmet into a referee's face because he was upset about a penalty call.
- In Hawaii, a high school soccer player tossed a referee to the ground because he'd been issued a yellow card.
- In Ohio, a junior high hockey player was charged with assault after punching a referee in the face, knocking him to the ground.

Why can't kids play by the rules? The rules are judgmental, and permissive parents make it even worse. They fully believe their children are perfect and always need to think they're winners. If they do lose, something must be wrong with the system, the coach, the referee—anyone and anything but their children.

- In Pennsylvania, a parent was criminally charged for biting a coach and shoving an official because his seven-year-old son lost a pee wee wrestling match.
- In Massachusetts, a dad was upset that the ten-year-old pickup game being supervised by an adult was "too rough," so he beat the supervisor to death in front of several of the children. He was found guilty of involuntary manslaughter.
- In North Carolina, the mother of a fourteen-year-old basketball player was given a "lifetime ban" after she jumped on the back of an official and scratched his face and neck.
- In New York, a father was charged with assault after allegedly using a hockey stick to bash his son's hockey coach because the coach didn't play his son in the final minute of the game.
- In Virginia, a mother slapped and scratched the face of a fifteen-year-old referee because she was upset about her nine-year-old's soccer game.
- In Indiana, parents began rioting at a youth football game after one parent hit a referee who was marking the ball out of bounds.

Where does this leave the coaches? In junior high and high school, they receive kids who don't know how to lose. Their parents expect them to win. The schools that often propagate the everyone-is-a-winner-all-the-time ideology at lower levels all of a sudden expect coaches to win for real. Coaches fear losing their jobs if they don't have a winning season.

- In Florida, a 270-pound youth football coach punched a referee because he thought the game of seven-year-olds was getting too rough. The coach had been penalized two times earlier in the game for unsportsmanlike behavior.
- In Oklahoma, a high school baseball coach allegedly attacked an umpire following the game.
- In New Mexico, a youth football coach punched a referee after disagreeing with a call during a title game for twelve- and thirteen-year-olds.

So to recap, kids are taught they never lose, and rules don't matter, and then they're taught they must win, and the rules do matter. The only logical way to never lose and always win is to cheat. So they do.

WHAT ARE YOUR KIDS LEARNING?

The state of sports and young athletes today is not an inspiring one. The Josephson Institute of Ethics, a nonprofit organization, conducted a survey of 5,275 high school athletes. The report, entitled "What Are Your Children Learning? The Impact of High School Sports on the Values and Ethics of High School Athletes," detailed the responses from 2005 and 2006. Michael Josephson, president of the organization, notes this in the report:

The bad news is that many coaches—particularly in the high profile sports of boys' basketball, baseball, and football—are teaching kids how to cheat and cut corners. In addition, far too many boys and girls engage in other dishonest, deceptive, and dangerous practices without regard for the rules or traditional notions of fair play and sportsmanship.[1]

Here is a fascinating find from the Josephson Institute study:

The vast majority of high school athletes say their coaches "consistently set a good example of ethics and character" (90 percent) and their current coach "wants them to do the ethically right thing, no matter what the cost."[2]

Keeping that in mind, the researchers then asked specific questions, but the answers fly in the face of what the kids originally stated. Here is where it gets really interesting:

- *Illegal holding*: 43 percent of the boys and 22 percent of girls think it's proper for a coach to teach basketball players how to illegally hold and push in ways that are difficult to detect (51 percent of football, 49 percent of baseball, and 47 percent of boys' basketball players agreed).
- *Using the other team's playbook*: 41 percent of the boys and 25 percent of the girls saw nothing wrong with using a stolen playbook sent in by an anonymous supporter before a big game. Baseball (49 percent) and football (48 percent) players were the most likely to approve of the use of the other team's playbook.
- *Faking an injury*: more than one in three of the boys and one in five of the girls think it's proper for a coach to instruct a player in football to fake an injury in order to get a needed time-out (44 percent of baseball and 43 percent of football players endorsed this strategy).
- *Illegally altering hockey stick*: 28 percent of boys in hockey said it was a proper part of the game for a hockey player to illegally alter a hockey stick.
- *Illegal start*: 28 percent of boys and 14 percent of girls approved of a soccer goalie deliberately violating the rules by moving forward three steps past the line on a penalty kick. The baseball and soccer

players were much more likely to endorse this practice: 37 percent of baseball players, 38 percent of boys' soccer players, and 18 percent of girls' soccer players.

- *Wrong players shooting free throws*: 25 percent of the boys and 13 percent of girls thought it was proper to try to trick a basketball referee by sending the wrong person to the line to shoot a free throw.
- *Altering the field of play*: building up the foul line—36 percent of baseball players said it was proper for a baseball coach to instruct a groundskeeper to build up the third-base foul line to help keep ground balls fair.
- *Soaking the field to slow down the other team*: 31 percent of the football players thought it was proper gamesmanship strategy for a football coach to instruct a groundskeeper to soak the field to slow down the opposing team.
- *Throwing at a batter*: 48 percent of baseball players and 10 percent of girls' softball players agreed it was a proper part of the game for a baseball coach to order his pitcher to throw at an opposing hitter in retaliation. Forty percent of baseball players and 20 percent of girls' softball players said it was acceptable for a softball pitcher to deliberately throw at a batter who hit a homerun the last time up.
- *Mistake in score*: 41 percent of boys and 23 percent of girls think it is acceptable for a volleyball coach to say nothing when an official makes a mistake in the score that favors their team.
- *Trash talk*: 42 percent of boys and 18 percent of girls approve of trash talk consisting of demeaning the defender's skill after every score.
- *Showboating*: 43 percent of boys and 33 percent of girls said it was acceptable for a player to do an elaborate *showboat* dance in front of the opponents' bench after scoring.
- *Motivation through insults*: 37 percent of boys and 13 percent of girls said it was okay for a coach to use profanity and personal insults to motivate players.
- *Swearing at an official to motivate the team*: 34 percent of boys and 12 percent of girls approved of a high school coach trying to pump up his team by swearing at the officials to get himself thrown out of the game.[3]

Remember, the kids told the researchers their coaches were "moral and ethical," meaning they obviously don't see cheating and unsportsmanlike behavior as immoral or unethical.

These statistics would indicate that kids are so willing to do anything to win that if a coach were to play by the rules and insist on fair and ethical behavior, even at the cost of winning a game, the players might quit. That is not true! The survey showed that the overwhelming majority of high school athletes value winning but would much rather *play* for a losing team than *sit on the bench* for a winning team. Further, they believe that winning is not essential for the enjoyment of the sport. Even on winning teams, as the young football player I discussed earlier in the chapter shows, there are kids who believe sportsmanship, fair play, and the game of the game are what matters. So how do they turn out that way? Without a doubt, it's because of how they are raised at home.

Any fool can criticize, condemn, and complain—and most fools do.

—DALE CARNEGIE

I always volunteer to drive my kids' sports teams, which helps me understand their ups and downs. If I hear the kids dumping on another child after a defeat, I can help turn the conversation to what the team can do to play better. It also offers an excellent opportunity to get to know the other children on the team, including what language is used in their homes and the character of the children. About 98 percent of the kids that have been in our van are really terrific, but you realize how quickly one or two negative children can start to hurt the whole group.

There was one boy on one of my son's basketball teams who seemed very quiet, even a little shy, whenever I'd see him at school. I actually felt a bit sorry for him and encouraged my son to try to befriend him. My son didn't like the boy, and I learned why when I went to their games.

First, the boy cheated and, when caught, would try to vigorously deny it.

Next, even though he was not a very good player, he would yell criticisms at his teammates while they were on the court. In huddles he would continue with a barrage of what others were doing wrong. Third, if a referee called a foul on him, he would start yelling at the referee and, sometimes using swear words, would argue that he hadn't done anything wrong even when the foul was so flagrant that he must have been aware of it. Fourth, if the team lost, he would loudly talk about how the opponents won only because they cheated, the ref was biased, or anything else that meant he was in no way responsible for the loss.

I wasn't even his mother, and I was mortified. I felt like apologizing on his behalf to the opposing team and their parents. It was disappointing that his coach didn't shut him down and stop the behavior. The coach did little more than tell him to stop yelling at the referee, and that was only after he'd done it a couple of times, and the ref threatened to kick him out of the game.

Why was he like this? He wasn't the biggest kid; he wasn't that coordinated. I think he was just so used to "being a winner" that he didn't know how to lose. When rules were enforced, he became angry to the point that he seemed barely able to control himself. Playing by the rules wasn't fair to him because that meant he wasn't always the winner. By never losing, you miss out on important lessons that will help you significantly later in life.

Nonpermissive parents realize the way for their children to build self-confidence and self-esteem is through hard work, which allows them to earn it on their own.

From B. T. in South Dakota:

I have been involved in youth activities for a very long time; church, scouts, school, and sports. On one of my soccer teams I had a couple of boys who acted out a lot. I talked to their parents about possible actions I could take. After some discussion one mom told me to have her son run laps. The other mom told me her son loves to run, and making him just sit somewhere would be punishment. Next practice they both started clowning around again. As per the agreements with their moms, one boy had to run while the other had to sit. Sure enough the boys argued to swap punishments. I held firm and the boys were much better behaved after that.

Good for B. T. and for those moms! Far too often, coaches have the opposite experience: parents lash out at the coach and worse. As professional sports came into the big-time, prime-time, mega-money position it enjoys today, the movement collided with a quote—a quote with a message the man who uttered it never intended: "Winning isn't everything; it's the only thing," said Vince Lombardi.

Did the Green Bay Packers' coach really mean that winning at all cost was more important than sportsmanship? No, in fact, not too long before his death, Lombardi said, "I wish %&* I'd never said the @*& thing. I meant the effort. I meant having a goal . . . I sure *#@ didn't mean for people to crush human values and morality." Since everyone repeats the former quote instead of the latter, Lombardi might have restated it to say, "Winning is wonderful, but sportsmanship is the lesson to retain for life." Truly, it is. It's a code that dictates behavior centered on the notion of fair play, hard work, and graciousness, regardless of whether you win or lose.

As a child, my sports idol was Roger Staubach, quarterback of the Dallas Cowboys. He was a man who exuded all the things that were right and good. He had a sterling reputation as a man of integrity. He was a fierce competitor with a solid work ethic. He was such a leader that, regardless of the score, you could see his team look at him and trust him to guide them through anything with victory as their goal. Many times they reached it, but even when they failed, he was again the person who set the example for the others to follow. He was gracious in a loss. He didn't look for others to blame. He didn't denigrate the opposing team or coach. He looked at himself to see what he could change to achieve the outcome he wanted. To me, he was John Wayne in a football uniform.

> *Courage is being scared to death, but saddling up anyway.*
>
> —JOHN WAYNE

Can you recall competing as a child? I played tennis, and as I got better, competing became scarier. To start with, the competition was tougher as you moved up the division rankings. I played for my school in the AA division. It's a lot less nerve rattling when you're playing your pals at the local court instead of being in front of a crowd, representing your school and playing for a trophy or ribbon.

My doubles partner was the niece of tennis legend Cliff Drysdale. Occasionally, he would coach us on the weekend. The sessions were notable for what he didn't teach. Contrary to recent tennis movies, where the main character analyzes how he can capitalize on the opponent's weakness, Cliff taught us to focus on our strengths and practice to make those strengths even better.

My parents were thrilled when we won district and supportive when we lost in the regionals. Their attitude really impacted my own. They weren't traumatized when I lost and didn't view it as a reflection of themselves. Boy, are some parents different from my own. A British newspaper reported on a mother who dedicated her life to her son's horse jumping shows. She was seen giving what she called "horse mints" to horses of other children in her son's division. People became suspicious when four of those horses tested positive for the doping agent acetylpromazine (ACP). Then the mother's veterinarian revealed that he'd given her four tablets containing ACP because she told him she needed them to sedate her son's horse for a clipping.

I'm not sure what happens to some parents. Do they think they are being judged based on how well their children perform in sports or in school? Do they feel that if they spend their time taking children to lessons or games, somehow they are owed a victory? Do they feel cheated or angry when their children or their teams don't win?

In this age of permissive parenting, the messages frequently sent to children are conflicting. Follow the progression in a young person's mind:

First, when they are young, they are told they are winners. Always. They can never lose, and they never do. When children play poorly, their parents spend even more time telling them how well they played.

Next, the children are in junior high. An official keeps score. The children realize people are now buying into this radical "points count" concept, which means someone will lose. But they've always been told they're winners. The children aren't prepared to handle defeat and aren't sure how their parents will react either. Their experiences show them that rules can be molded to fit the goal.

When they hit high school and college, the coach's job security is often based on the team record. Technically, there are rules, but they've been taught they have to be winners, so cheating to win is fine since the rules were selectively used earlier. In college, the Bowl Championship Series (BCS) sports rating system rewards what I consider to be unsportsmanlike conduct. Running up the score on a team pushes the winning team higher up the ladder. As a graduate of the University of Texas (and as much as I love my alma mater), I find it embarrassing when the Longhorns run up the score against another team. The BCS system rewards an easy win instead of a hard-fought win. The lesson to student athletes is that crushing, demolishing an opponent, even if they are vastly inferior, is expected and proper conduct.

WHEN THE FINAL WHISTLE BLOWS

In the final analysis, when it comes to sports, here are the lessons Joe and I teach our kids:

1. They aren't winners every time, but they have the *chance* to win every time if they practice and do their best.
2. They must be respectful of the referees and all coaches.
3. They must encourage others, and any statements to teammates must be constructive in word and tone.
4. They must take responsibility for their actions without excuses.
5. They should show appreciation for the good effort of others even if they are opposing players.
6. They should exhibit good sportsmanship at all times.

Taking an active role in your child's sports gives you a perfect classroom to teach life lessons. You are in a positive, fun environment. Touchy, feely child psychologists will tell you it's important to make every child feel like a winner and that by never losing children will grow up feeling empowered and self-confident. It's a great theory, but it doesn't work that way in reality. Losing at something early in life is a wonderful lesson. Your children learn how to face failure and bounce right back. They realize that it's not the end of the world but simply a natural event. At some point everyone loses at something, and the earlier your child learns how to do it and keep right on trying, the better prepared he will be to lead a happy life.

Our greatest weakness lies in giving up. The most certain way to succeed is always to try just one more time.

—THOMAS A. EDISON

The Dress Code

I base my fashion taste on what doesn't itch.
—GILDA RADNER

My first inkling that parenthood was going to be a bit more challenging than I had imagined came when I was living in New York City. Laurel was three and Matt was two. Both went to the 92nd Street Y nursery school about four blocks from our apartment. To get there we walked by a very exclusive prep school.

The school has a solid reputation for being competitive to gain entrance. Parents work very hard to ensure they have enough people pulling for their children so that they get an acceptance. Children graduate from there and move into top-rated colleges. Later in life they are frequently the movers and shakers in New York City. I knew of the school's reputation and was fairly speechless when I walked by the school for the first time. Let me set the scene.

We lived at 89th and Park Avenue, and the school was directly around the corner. As I pushed the stroller down the street, the first sensation was the overwhelming smell of cigarettes. As I looked down the street, I saw the door steps, or stoops, of the brownstone townhouses were packed with children sporting cigarettes dangling from between their lips. Huge puffs in, eyes pinched, and after a pause, the smoke billows back out of their mouths.

The next unexpected sight was the fashion accessories. Keep in mind that these are kids between the ages of fourteen and eighteen. The girls were decked out in a very obvious way—that shiny, big, "look at me; I'm expensive," Chanel-earrings kind of way. Their thousand-dollar Chanel purses were tossed carelessly on the ground near their cigarette packs. The girls looked like women, hard and jaded women. It was not what I expected to see outside such a posh school. Of course, I'm sure there were plenty of regular kids inside the school, but this was what you saw hanging around outside.

PICK YOUR BATTLES?

We parents are told that we should "pick our battles" with our kids. The experts tell us to skip some issues that on their surface may not seem that important but are an integral part of your child's development. While that's true, some of the battles they don't consider important really are when you look more closely and when you're the parent of the child in question and must live with the consequences.

Permissive parents rationalize that making mistakes and learning from them are part of growing up. Nonpermissive parents know kids will make mistakes, but they are willing to take the time to try to influence their children's choices to steer them away from choices that could haunt them. When a parent opts out of his role, peers move in to fill the void. They don't have to live with the mistakes, though; you do.

Your child's outward appearance is a favorite battleground. Yes, fads come and go, and if you simply wait, your child will pass through them, but not all fads and not all kids. Why gamble with your child? There are plenty of other areas where children can practice decision making and gain independence. What people see on the outside is what they expect to find on the inside. If your child dresses like a thug, people will assume he is a thug. If he dresses in a presentable fashion, people may not assume he's a great kid, but they certainly won't start out with negative opinions that he would have to overcome.

> *Live so that you wouldn't be ashamed*
> *to sell the family parrot to the town gossip.*
>
> —WILL ROGERS

New York City is one of the hubs of permissive parenting. Paris Hilton is the prime example. At the age of fifteen, she was already a staple in the *New York Post* gossip section for reportedly dancing on tables while not wearing any underwear. Very soon after that, her numerous sexual escapades began to be detailed. Not surprisingly, her alleged sexually transmitted diseases (STDs) were gossiped about at great length. You might think this would cause parents in the city to keep a tighter rein on their children. Just the opposite. It seemed they were just fine with their own children racing toward ill repute and lifelong health issues.

So why would wealthy, well-educated parents allow daughters to chain-smoke while lounging on door steps dressed like tramps with money? I think of the quote by Carol Gustav Jung about the unlived life of a parent being a stronger psychological influence on his children than anything else.

Perhaps these parents thought they missed out on something in their own teen years. Perhaps they always wished they had designer earrings at fifteen, and so, because they are now able to, they buy them for their own children. Perhaps their own parents didn't let them stay out in bars until three in the morning while they were in high school, so now they're letting their children do it. It's frightening and pathetic to see parents trying to live vicariously through their children.

I had an acquaintance around this time in my apartment building. The younger of her two children had been born in the past year, and she was unable to stick to a diet to take off the baby weight. Oddly enough, her apartment was packed with junk food. She, though, would go to great lengths to try not to eat it. Instead, she would feed it to her children. *Feed* isn't quite the right term. It was similar to what I expect happens to a duck that becomes foie gras. They were stuffed with junk food. I guess psychologically she was either trying to make her children big too, or because she wasn't supposed to eat the junk food, she got something out of watching her kids eat it. Either way, it was detrimental to mother and children.

Can you imagine anyone having made fun of the old Farrah Fawcett hairdo when you consider what you see on people's heads today? Dealing with clothing that kids wear is tough, but at least they can take it off. When they dye their hair or get it cut, it lasts a *lot* longer! Take my stepdaughter, who is beautiful. Really, she's truly striking. She is six foot one with perfect, pale skin and beautifully thick and shiny auburn hair. Or, at least, that's the way it *was* before she dyed it coal black. Goth black. Black . . . like the color of the room after we passed out from shock.

What would make a gorgeous girl do something to make herself look less attractive? I think a bit of the-grass-is-always-greener-on-the-other-side thinking came into play. Not to mention, some friends told her it would look good, and she admired someone else who had black hair; you know, logical stuff. We tried to explain to her—as tactfully as possible—that when you have hair as stunning as hers, you just don't mess with it. She, of course, thinks her hair is "brown and boring." A person can't simply come straight out and say, "Wow! Does that make you look *ugly*," especially when dealing with a stepdaughter. Instead, my husband and I pointed out that black hair on people with her skin color tends to make them look ashen.

Although teens are loath to agree with you about anything, it turned out she wasn't really happy with the color either. So we looked forward to the next weekend we had her and hoped that maybe the color would have begun to wash out. Nope. Instead, she'd gotten blond highlights on *top* of the black hair! If you're a hairstylist, I'm sure you're already wincing. I don't think *anyone* has successfully pulled that combination off. This case was no exception. The blond turned out looking like ashes from the fireplace and made the black look even more severe. Cruella DeVil anyone? At this point, we just kept quiet and prayed she wouldn't try a bright orange Mohawk! It took a few more months and a couple more dye jobs, but she finally went back to her natural color by and by.

I agree with the advice that parents should pick their battles. We figured

that since it wasn't permanent—and however unattractive, it wasn't distract-
ing—we'd just let her come around in her own time.

GIRLS, GIRLS, GIRLS

One morning recently I was greeted by the most wonderful sight in years. My
daughter Laurel was trying on the uniform for her new school, the Hockaday
School in Dallas. *Thank you, my dear Lord!* I couldn't contain my glee. I'd opened
the box when the uniform arrived and couldn't wait to see it on her. I actually
heard Laurel before I saw her. Her footsteps—or perhaps foot *stomps* is a better
way to characterize it—indicated there was something wrong. She opened the
door to my den—using that grand whooshing motion, similar to a diva about
to enter the stage. Then she cocked one foot sideways, put her hands on her
hips, and said (with attitude), "You've gotta be kidding." I had always visualized
her looking like this but never expected my fantasy to become reality.

Let me describe the look toe to head: it begins with 1950s green-and-
white saddle shoes and bobby socks (although the girls are allowed to wear
knee socks if they want to cover more leg). The green-and-white plaid pleated
skirt falls about an inch below the knee. The stiff, white cotton button-down
shirts seem to come from a plus-size store, and the shirt is covered by an
equally, let's call it, "roomy" green cardigan. I was itching to put her hair in
pigtails with white bows.

I gushed, "You look adorable!" Wrong thing to say to a teenage girl. They
do not want to look adorable these days. They want to look *hot*. The only way
to achieve a hot look in this uniform was if you were sweating.

Laurel was on the verge of tears, begging me to please see if there were any
way to hem the skirt shorter. The school said that, yes, it could be hemmed
to two inches above her knee. By today's standards that's still a granny skirt.
I love it. I immediately grabbed my camera and took a picture to send to her
grandmothers.

Frankly, I think every school, private and public, should have a uniform.
It's less expensive for families, and it removes the daily battles with kids over

their clothing. It's also wonderful for children. They don't have to worry if their family can't afford the latest fashions. They will be judged on who they are instead of what they wear.

Go to most public schools in America and you'll see questionable slogans on T-shirts, ripped jeans, baseball caps on sideways. I've had a very easy time with Matt. I bought him his first pair of blue jeans when he was a young boy—good, durable dungarees, as my dad would say. They were also stiff as a board. In fact, that one pair that was purchased for Matt was then worn by one brother and four cousins. It's now being worn by my youngest son. The blue jean material has softened up now, but the initial discomfort led to Matt refusing to wear jeans until he turned fourteen this year and asked me to buy him a *soft* pair. After a great deal of searching, I finally found one I was willing to pay the price tag for at Kohl's department store. Do you have any idea how much a *worn* pair of jeans costs? Seriously, one of the teenage girls asked for a specific pair for Christmas. I went to an outlet store where they were "marked down" to just under two hundred dollars . . . for blue jeans! No, she did not get them. I told her the saying that's been attributed to everyone from P. T. Barnum to Mark Twain, "A sucker is born every minute."

Don't get me wrong; I don't want my kids to be ridiculed, but I won't spend money foolishly. If you live near a large city, tear out the stories from the newspaper that you will inevitably see about teens being stabbed, shot, and even killed for their tennis shoes. How can any parent or society allow so much value to be placed on what a kid wears? I use those stories to highlight inappropriate values. As a street reporter in New York City, I often covered the crime beat. I can tell you in all honesty that I saw children in Section Eight housing, which is for the poorest of the poor, in outfits with designer logos that cost several hundred dollars—more money than the entire month's rent for their parents' apartment. What is the message?

Teenage girls are a handful without adding the stress of what they want to wear. I recall being in my seventh-grade sewing class and making an A-line skirt. It was twenty-one inches long, and my dad thought I had hemmed it too short. I told him he had old-fashioned taste and that I'd never wear a skirt longer than twenty-one inches.

He said, "Okay, sign a promise note." He wrote a note with my statement and had me sign it. Of course, it was just one year later when fashionable skirt lengths became longer, and he pulled out the note. I learned a lot then about making unqualified statements. I still have the note as a reminder. Between that time and now, Madonna and then Britney Spears came on the scene, and even marginally presentable girl's clothing went into the trash. Skirts aren't just short; they are so tight they have to be made of stretch material. Blouses were put into the dryer on high heat, and some knucklehead decided even five-year-old girls should wear shoes with heels. Even baby clothing became sexualized. Baby shirts declare "I'm a hottie." Excuse me? Let me clue you in. It's tough enough dealing with girls' sexuality when they hit teenage years. The last thing any wise parent wants to do is start declaring her daughter is sexy when she's six months old.

BOYS WILL BE BOYS

Boys are another story. You don't have to worry about them wearing shorts that are too short or showing too much cleavage, but that doesn't mean you are home free. People make assumptions based on how a boy dresses because, just like girls, boys wear certain clothing to make a particular statement. As a parent, you must decide if the statement is appropriate or sometimes even decent.

> *When I was a boy of fourteen, my father was*
> *so ignorant I could hardly stand to have the old man*
> *around. But when I got to be twenty-one, I was astonished*
> *at how much the old man had learned in seven years.*
>
> —JOSH BILLINGS

About a year ago, Collin decided he wanted to be a magician. At least that's what I thought because he was intent on having his pants defy gravity.

I thought there might actually be a secret set of suspenders underneath his shirt, holding his waistband in a sort of no-man's-land between his thigh and his knees. While his underwear is always clean, we still didn't think it was decent for anyone and his mother to be able to see half of his underwear before getting to his pants. We told him to pull them up. He did, but they kept slipping back down. When we'd bought him new pants, he'd asked for a size too large (I think to more easily effect this look).

He pled innocent: "I really don't want to wear them like that. I had you buy a larger size so they would last longer."

We went right along with it, saying, "That's good thinking. So for now, wear a belt so they'll stay up."

The belt never materialized. I told him the next time I caught him beltless with his pants inching toward terra firma, I would help them along the way. I guess he didn't believe me because the next day the belt was nowhere to be found. So while walking down the main street in our town, which is always packed with people, I walked up behind him and gave a quick tug. Down came the pants! Up went the eyebrows in shock that I'd actually followed through. But guess what? He's remembered a belt ever since then.

> *By the time a man realizes that maybe his father was right,*
> *he usually has a son who thinks he's wrong.*
>
> —CHARLES WADSWORTH

I was struck by how far society's expectations of boys had slipped when I read a flyer sent home by our son's summer camp. They attend Camp Stewart in Hunt, Texas. It's the oldest boys' camp in the Southwest, and the values it started out with in 1924 are the exact same values they continue to teach campers today. But apparently, the camp's job has become harder over the decades, which is why it found it helpful to mail this flyer to parents. It's a want ad from early last century:

Boy Wanted

A boy that stands straight, sits straight, acts straight, and talks straight;

A boy whose fingernails are not in mourning, whose ears are clean, whose clothes are clean, and whose hair is combed;

A boy who listens carefully when he is spoken to, who asks questions when he does not understand, and does not ask questions about things that are none of his business;

A boy who is polite to every man and respectful to every woman and girl;

A boy who does not smoke cigarettes and has no desire to learn how;

A boy who is more eager to know how to speak good English than to talk slang;

A boy that never bullies other boys nor allows other boys to bully him;

A boy who, when he does not know a thing, says "I don't know," and when he makes a mistake says, "I'm sorry," and when he is asked to do something says, "I'll try";

A boy who looks you straight in the eye and tells the truth every time;

A boy who would rather lose his job or be expelled from school than to tell a lie or be a cad;

A boy who other boys like;

A boy who is at ease in the company of girls;

A boy who is not sorry for himself and not forever thinking and talking about himself;

A boy who makes you feel good when he is around;

A boy who is not a goody-goody or a little prig, but is healthy, happy, and full of life.

This boy is wanted everywhere. The family wants him, the school wants him, the office wants him, the boys want him, the girls want him, all creation wants him.

That kind of boy is not easy to create, but how different our society would be if more parents were able to accomplish it. If you listen to the permissive parenting experts, they'll tell you the child's choice—even when in sharp contrast to the above-mentioned behavior and dress—is what is most important to his development.

MAKING CHOICES

Permissive-parenting experts will tell you that children are adults in the making. Factually, that's true. But far too often the "in the making" part is forgotten, and children are given more control than they are able to handle. The experts will tell you that by exerting control over your children, you are denying them the freedom that we value so much in our society. "What message will that send to them?" they fret. They will tell you to let your children make the decisions for themselves because it's their right as human beings. Have you ever noticed that the permissive-parenting experts have a very selective list of what rights children do and don't have? There are schools on the East Coast where a student can't take an aspirin without the school getting written permission from the parent. However, if that child wants to get birth control pills or an abortion, somehow the whole parental-permission thing goes out the window. How crazy is that? We have a responsibility to our children not to give rights and control to them before we equip them to handle it.

> *What the people believe is true.*
>
> —ANISHINABE INDIAN PROVERB

These adults in the making are *young* people with undeveloped brains and a lack of experience to intelligently make many choices. Here is a not-uncommon scenario.

A teenager, let's call him Max, arrives at a new school. He has a strange haircut dyed in a color not found in nature, wears black punk-rock T-shirts, and sports a nose ring. Inside, Max is a responsible, intelligent, caring young man, but his outward appearance says the opposite.

Max wants to makes friends and fit in at his new school. The kids see him and wonder what issue is he dealing with. Their parents view Max and think they don't want their kids to socialize with Max because he will be a bad influence. Remember when your parents would say to you, "You are not allowed to see so-and-so because he [or she] is a bad influence"? They rarely came to that conclusion based on knowing so-and-so as a person; their decision was often just because they thought the person *looked* like trouble.

In school, teachers take one look at a kid like Max and also assume he's a troublemaker. The bottom line is that while it's great to give children choices, there are some significant consequences they simply don't think about or don't realize are important. That means they are unable to make an informed decision based on life experiences. If Max had nonpermissive parents, they would have told him that his unique choice of hair fashion would stand out, resulting in his having trouble meeting people because they and their parents would get the wrong impression. Further, teachers would make negative assumptions that Max would have to work very hard to overcome. If parents explain their decisions, children realize that their parents love them and are taking the time to think through what will help their children be as successful as they want to be. Nonpermissive parents help their children steer clear of unnecessary roadblocks to their long-term happiness, instead of sloughing off their duty and telling their children to "do what feels right."

I guarantee that if you go to any school in America and find the group of kids who fit the description of Max, they will be the kids who have permissive parents—whom, by the way, they likely don't talk to. Few of them perform well in school, and the popular kids who run the school generally want nothing to do with them. Permissive parents think they are raising liberated young people by allowing their children to make free decisions about everything, but instead, they set up the children to become outcasts. After their children are grown, they will wonder why their parents didn't care enough about them to save them from themselves.

Our teenage daughter, Jordan, absolutely disagrees with me about this section. She says high school kids are going to be eighteen and able to make their own decisions soon enough, so parents should start letting them make mistakes and learn from them now. If they don't, she argues, they'll do it after they leave home. She also makes the argument that it's wrong and unfair for people to judge others without even knowing them. At this point during our discussion, I grab a cup of coffee and sit down, realizing this is a perfect opportunity for a heart-to-heart. Joe, who is sitting at the table nearby, pulls the newspaper up higher—clearly he is happy to let me handle this one.

I say, "Hey, welcome to the world! That's life. People make assumptions based on the way you look."

And it's true. I do it; you do it; Jordan does it. Given enough time, people might get to know the *real* Max and realize he isn't some nutcase, but why force him to work overtime just to get an even break? That's what this is about. Children need freedom; they need to be able to make choices, but that also needs to occur within boundaries that will help them make smarter choices, choices they will be thankful for later.

Jordan argues that it doesn't matter if Max's choices lead to false impressions that hold him back because, she says, it's only high school, and he has his whole life in front of him.

My response is yes, but the choices made in high school impact where you go to college, which frequently impacts what firm or company hires you after school. The basic premise is that you can show your individuality, freedom of expression, and creativity without piercing your nose and wearing a Mohawk. If you feel like moving to a remote region and living in a cave, you don't need to be able to function in society, but unless that's your plan, you'd better realize that society will form opinions—positive or negative—and those will help or hurt you. (She still thinks Max isn't a nutcase . . . and wants his cell number.)

I recently was discussing this exchange with a professor from Stanford University. He told me he made the deal with his daughters that he would provide the down payments on their first homes if they hadn't pierced anything but their ears at that point. Then he shared an even more interesting story.

A fellow professor, who was quite liberal, had told this man that his views were backward. He urged him to let his daughter make any choice she wanted. That was how he was raising his college-age son. The boy was into tattooing, and the dad said the number of imprints on his son's body was growing, but, "Hey, he's a kid. He'll grow out of it."

Flash forward three years. He did grow out of the phase, but now he was trying to get a job. He was smart, had gone to a great college, but no one at the corporations where he was applying was willing to hire him. Why? His tattoos were in many places that he couldn't cover up with clothing, including his neck and hands. His appearance didn't sync with the image of the corporations.

His dad summed up that the only place his son's look would fit in was at a tattoo parlor or, perhaps, an automotive garage where he would deal with cars, not people. He told my friend that he only now realized what a great disservice he'd done his son by not helping him steer clear of poor choices that seem fine at nineteen but haunt you soon after.

General Douglas MacArthur once said this:

Build me a son, O Lord, who will be strong enough to know when he is weak, and brave enough to face himself when he is afraid; one who will be proud and unbending in honest defeat, and humble and gentle in victory. Give him humility, so that he may always remember the simplicity of true greatness, the open mind of true wisdom, and the meekness of true strength. Then I, his father, will dare to whisper, "I have not lived in vain."[1]

Boys, while easier to raise in some ways, can still be pretty tough. Take their hair. I know I'm not being fair, but there are just certain judgments I'm going to make when I see a child with a shaved head except for a small braid trailing the length of his neck. When a kid has long hair—and by long I mean you can't see his eyes—a little voice in the back of my head whispers, "Trouble!"

When my eldest nephew, Andrew, made a visit to attend a weeklong football camp with a couple of our boys, I picked him up from the airport. I couldn't help myself and blurted out, "Wow, is your hair long!" I mean, it was such a departure from his Christmas card photo. And they were going to football camp in ninety-three-degree weather; he would sweat to death with that mop on his head!

Andrew's dad is a perpetually well-groomed airline pilot, and he quickly offered me free rein with Andrew's hair. I took him up on the offer. The next day after I returned from work, Andrew accompanied me to the back porch, and I started snipping away. I was very matter-of-fact about it. Secretly, I think I'm a frustrated barber. When Andrew began protesting that boys in his town don't wear their hair short, I replied that I wasn't cutting it short, but rather to a normal length. He sat there fuming, but he didn't say a thing. It's easier to complain and argue with your mom, but it's tougher with your aunt. He didn't know how far he could push it, so he just sat there. *Snip. Snip. Snip.* I thought at one point he was going to cry, but after a bit, the lip quivering stopped. I called my sister, and she told me that she'd been having an impossible time getting him to the barber shop.

The next day, I took Andrew to my office where my lifesaver hairstylist was waiting. I didn't tell Andrew about it ahead of time. I just plopped him in the chair and told him that while I tried my best, there had been so much hair to cut that I may not have done a perfect job. I explained that my hairstylist would fix anything that needed adjusting. Then I walked out. Now, Andrew had never met my hairstylist, so he wasn't about to start arguing with a six-foot-four man with a twinkle in his eye and scissors in his hand. Andrew sat there while the hairstylist took a bit more off.

He looked so handsome. I told him the girls would be chasing him so much he'd have to beat them off with a stick. He was still a bit upset, but cooled off, and my sister totally owes me one! He does too. At camp this summer, he got a date for every one of the dances. He's very proud of it too!

Children aren't happy with nothing to ignore,
and that's what parents were created for.

—OGDEN NASH

We are having an issue with one of our fourteen-year-old boys, Collin. It is one of those battles that the experts would probably say to ignore, but I disagree. Collin is a bright kid, good grades, and plays in the band. When we were in Austin, Texas recently, we visited a Boat Town dealership, and Collin wanted a baseball cap. It was emblazoned with some company's wakeboarding logo. It looked fine enough.

Then he put it on, cocked sideways and high on his head. I've seen the look on rap musicians. I took the cap and straightened it and said that backwards or forwards was the only way he was wearing it. About five minutes later he had taken it off and put it back on . . . sideways. This time Joe fixed it. Collin still hasn't given up, and neither do we. He'll tire of it eventually.

I know that how a boy wears his cap simply isn't very important, but the message it sends is. You want your children to have every opportunity possible. At the beginning of a race, why let them start ten paces back? They have to work that much harder just to get even, let alone win the race.

WHAT DRESS CODE?

It's tough getting dressed these days. Even adults are having trouble. What exactly do you wear to an event that specifies "Dressy Business Casual"? Huh? In the 1990s companies began adapting dress-down policies. It started with casual Fridays; then, with the Silicon Valley boom, casual attire seemed to spread like the waistband on Dockers pants. In New York City, where the advertising and music industries end the summer workweek at noon on Friday at the latest, top executives began wearing their cargo shorts and J. Crew flip-flops to work.

> *Women's fashion is a euphemism*
> *for fashion created by men for women.*
>
> —ANDREA DWORKIN

As work attire changed, so did church attire. Remember wearing your "Sunday finest"? In some churches, that now could be a bikini. Honestly, there are people who gather for Sunday service by tethering their boats together. We happen to attend a church where people frequently wear shorts and T-shirts. One lady, who is always up front doing a lot of the hand waving during song service, seems to be wearing bike shorts, so she may be riding two wheels to service. Our congregation, which is looking for a lot to build a new sanctuary, gathers in a school auditorium that doesn't have air-conditioning, so there really is a reason for the lack of coats and ties, but I still think biking shorts goes a bit too far. The clothing world is pretty hard to sort out these days.

While the initial dress-down concept was thought to free creativity and make people more productive because they were more comfortable, it didn't necessarily work out that way. Recent studies have found that when people dressed more casually, they began treating work and deadlines more casually too. In the past few years, we've seen a swing in the pendulum, and the dress code is tightening its belt. Older kids and young adults are confused. What is appropriate?

At one television station where I worked, an intern arrived one morning dressed in shiny black shorts (short ones), a white T-shirt, and pumps. Talk about schizophrenia. Perhaps she wanted to be prepared for any option, including going to a disco or a pickup tennis game. She may have been a great worker, but the impression she made on everyone and her lack of professionalism displayed by her attire is all we remembered each time we saw her after that.

I will never forget how one new hire, a recent college graduate, went out to greet a former secretary of state and escort him to the television studio. She was wearing what looked like a beach cover-up and flip-flops! Unfortunately, no one saw her when she arrived at work or before this happened. When the show's producer came to say hello to the guest, he saw what she was wearing. A stern discussion followed.

I figured out a way to head this off with my interns. They are usually college juniors and come from all over the country. Frequently, this is their first major corporate work experience. On the first day I have two of my friends pull the young person aside. They explain how wonderful my former interns have been. They detail how most of them were hired by news broadcasters right after graduation. Why? I am particular and expect my interns to be the brightest, hardest-working, and best-dressed because they are a reflection of me and my show. One of my friends will then run through the don'ts:

Don't . . .

1. *Wear flip-flops.* Short of working at a beach or pool, they are not appropriate, besides being a bit unhygienic. They also highlight a feature that is rarely a person's best. How often do you hear someone say, "Did you see Jane's toes? Wow, I wish mine looked like that"? Never. Almost *no one* has beautiful toes. And guys generally don't think to clip their nails until they come close to ripping one off. Yick!

2. *Show too much skin.* You know what kind I mean. What is acceptable in a workplace is best judged by seeing how most of the employed women there dress. Yes, looking hot will get someone noticed, but it may also keep that person from getting a full-time job once out of college.

3. *Show piercing and tattoos.* I know it's fashionable in the younger set, but I promise you will not find many corporate leaders wearing nose rings to the office. In the office, when a girl bends down and reveals a tattoo just above her behind, everyone assumes that is simply the start. People make assumptions.

My husband has had interns whom he can't allow to attend meetings because they would hurt business. Many of his firm's clients are from other countries. Oddly enough, since tattoos are evidenced on Japanese clay figurines dating from 300 BC or older, he says Asian businesspeople are particularly put off by tattoos on business professionals. Since most large corporations are doing a bulk of business with firms from Asia, tattoos can create a real issue.

We wonder what these young adults will be saying to themselves in a few years. Remember Angelina Jolie's body art? She committed a tattoo no-no. Never put a person's name or likeness on your body. I love *Tomb Raider*, but it's impossible to miss the makeup artist's noble but ineffective attempt to hide

Jolie's tattoo of her former husband's name. Even though they attempted to dig-
itally remove it frame by frame, "Billy Bob" kept coming through the makeup
and simply stood out on a character who was ostensibly a British aristocrat. I
think she's attempted to have it taken off since. Ouch. Rule of thumb: don't do
it where you can't hide it. Ditto for piercing. When it goes beyond your ears,
keep it behind fabric.

Do . . .

1. *Arrive at work on time.* One of my former producers had to
   speak to an intern who simply arrived at the office late many, if
   not most, days. While the girl had talent and was quite nice, she
   did not make a good professional impression on the people to
   whom she would likely apply in order to get a job after college.

2. *Plan to work hard, or else don't apply for work at all.* Again, I have an
   intern story I will never forget. People who hire you rely on your
   being there and working diligently. An extremely hardworking and
   accomplished friend of mine had a daughter who was interested
   in an internship. She attended one of the best universities in the
   country, her writing was solid, and her academic record was stellar.
   I thought she'd be terrific. And she may have been if she had ever
   shown up. In her first week, she explained that she'd planned a trip
   a long time ago, so she would be gone for the next two weeks. She
   returned, but even later than she had said, and then worked another
   week before taking off again for another fully paid-for trip planned
   long ago. It was hard for me to reconcile how she could have such a
   hardworking parent yet seem unable to comprehend the basic concept that if you have a job, you show up for work. I tell the story
   about her to prospective interns and tell them if that's the type of job
   they dream of, they need to find somewhere else to work.

3. *Dress like the person whose job you want.* Most interns want the
   job their boss has. If they look the part, they have a better chance
   of getting the part. Good or bad, it's more likely that an average
   person who presents himself well will get a promotion before a

brilliant person who looks like a beach bum gets one. Few college kids have an unlimited bank account, but there are numerous off-price or outlet stores that offer professional clothing at a very reasonable price. They just have to make the choice to buy a gray suit instead of another pair of low-rise jeans.

A WEIGHTY ISSUE

An estimated maximum of 10 percent of adults have eating disorders. Some 66 percent of adults in America, about 134 million people, are overweight or obese according to the National Health and Nutrition Examination Survey from 2001 to 2004. They don't all of a sudden become overweight adults. These people are born as normal, healthy kids, but then they start to grow and grow and grow. By the time they're adults, they are frustrated by diets they don't stick to. They get used to the way they look and feel as fat adults, and they glance around them and see a lot of people just like them, or even larger, and justify their size.

From 1960 to 2004, the prevalence of obesity has skyrocketed. For some reason, the statistics show that we are getting bigger; yet, it seems that the hot topics on TV and in magazines are anorexia, too-skinny models, and why people should feel good about having overweight bodies. Of course anorexia should be taken seriously. But it is estimated just 1 to 3 percent of teenage girls suffer from eating disorders, such as anorexia or bulimia, whereas at least 17 percent of teenagers are overweight.

Faced with these facts, which of these do you think is the worse problem? It doesn't appear that we face a *skinny* epidemic. Still, more focus seems to be on the smaller issue. A complaint we hear is that the fashion and advertising industries set us up to hold false expectations. We are told that they have evil agendas to parade stick-thin models down catwalks so that we feel bad about the way we look. We are told that their aim is to coerce us into dieting until we can look just like their models do. Maybe I'm in the minority, but I realize I will never be six feet tall and perfectly proportioned. Further, I certainly don't aspire to look like a runway model.

I also have an interesting story to share about today's models, which flies in the face of what you usually hear. The change may have occurred after the "Milan melee" when it was declared that models who did not have a healthy body mass index (BMI) would not be allowed on the runway. It's a great idea, and by the time the shows hit New York, you could see healthier bodies.

Our oldest daughter, Jordan, recently was spotted by an agent for Elite, which is one of the top modeling agencies in the world. With her height she's hard to miss. When she went in for her meeting with the head of the runway division, she was told she needed to lose weight. I can't tell you what she weighed because I want her to continue to talk to me, but her measurements were 36-26-38, and they wanted her to get her thighs to 36. They stressed, though, that they did *not* want her to lose too much weight because then the clothes wouldn't look good. The emphasis, in contradiction to the stereotype, was for her to be a healthy weight and fit.

When people begin talking about how everyone is focused on skinniness, I think back to my mother's heyday. Women had waistlines that were the size of my thigh. Those poodle skirts looked as cute as they did because of girls' tiny waists, which anchored the flounced, flared skirts that would spread out like waffle-edged paper plates when they were "Rockin' Around the Clock." The icons of the day, Katherine Hepburn, Bette Davis, and Angela Lansbury, were thin. But no one was accusing *them* of setting up false expectations for women's self-images.

The greatest change since that time is that women today are much less proportionate. In 1960 the average woman's height, according to the National Center for Health Statistics at the Center for Disease Control, was 5'3". Since then, the average height has increased only one inch to 5'4". Meanwhile, the same is not true with our weight. The average woman in 1960 weighed 144 pounds. Today she weighs 152 pounds. The age group that shows the greatest gain in that period of time is women aged 20 to 29. We're getting fatter at a time in our lives when we should be the most physically fit. Why? I hear a lot of excuses.

Here's what drives me nuts. My mother is beautiful in that classic, beauty-queen sort of way. In fact, she was a college beauty queen at Drake University, received modeling offers from New York, and movie offers from Hollywood. Now, if there were a sweet tooth, our family would own it. We *love* sugar: cakes, cookies, pies, and anything chocolate. Honestly, I've thought numerous times that I would never, ever need to think about my weight if I could just find a hypnotist who could make me believe I don't love sweets.

Sometime in her early forties, after she'd had three children, my mom, who had been fit all her life, started to put on weight. All of us kids could see that she was eating the same yummy stuff, but she was exercising less. After a bit of yo-yo dieting, she started telling us her weight gain was genetic. Granted, our grandmother was exceptionally overweight. But I've also seen pictures of her at a young age, and she was fit at that stage too. There was just some point at which everyone in our family started putting on weight but stopped doing what they needed to do in order to remain fit. I always thought that if the cause of our family weight gain was genetic, why did it start well into adulthood? One Christmas, I paid for my mom and dad to join Nutrisystem. Within about six months, they had lost their extra weight and were much more active. They were proud of their accomplishment, and they looked and felt great. For my dad's sixty-fifth birthday, I got him a wakeboard, and he actually used it!

I've been there too. Flashback to me at age seventeen. I had just finished my first year of college, and my cheeks were chubby. Remember that period in your life? You are away from home for the first time, eating whatever you choose; and in my case, drinking all the soda pop I wanted. Then it happens: you pack on that infamous "freshman 15" in no time. It's no myth. It's a reality . . . I would know!

I came home after that first year, and my dad said, "Well, you're just big boned."

What? How did I—all of a sudden, mind you—go from being the Junior Miss of Dripping Springs (okay, so there weren't that many people in the competition) to being big boned? My dad was trying to be sweet and say something kind, as he always did, which is an admirable trait but not always the most honest one. In reality I was . . . well, let's go with "chunky." I put the first five pounds on in my cheeks (the ones in my face, that is).

It took my brutally honest high school biology teacher, Mrs. Huffman, to tell me I was fat and needed to lose weight. As I recall, she put it like this:

"What did you do, swallow a cow?" Yes, maybe she was a bit too blunt, but she forced me to question my dad's creative reasoning and face the truth. I started exercising and dieting. I eventually lost the weight, and I respect Mrs. Huffman to this day for caring about me enough to be straight with me.

AN EXCEPTION TO THE RULES

While Mrs. Huffman never had children of her own, she certainly raised a lot of children. Perhaps because she didn't have kids, she wasn't encumbered by all the parenting advice of the era. She just did what she thought was right after all those years of teaching. If she saw someone dressed inappropriately, she would say something about the impression that person was making. She never did that in a condescending manner or with a harsh tone; she'd usually rely on a bit of humor and joking to get the message through. If she saw someone putting on weight, as a biology teacher she would talk to that person about the health implications.

Kids adored her. She was a straight shooter, an adult who cared about them, and because of that, an adult that hundreds of students loved as their own parent.

Mrs. Huffman recently applied for a burial plot at a public cemetery in our town, but she had moved outside the town limits. So many former students wrote letters to the cemetery board describing how she had helped raise them to become the people they are today, that the board made an exception for her.

If you follow her example as a parent, your kids will adore you too. Just do what you believe is right—be an exception to the rules of permissive parenting.

Trust yourself; you know more than you think you do.

—Dr. Benjamin Spock

Teenagers: The Alien Years

*Few things are more satisfying than seeing your
own children have teenagers of their own.*

—Doug Larson

My sons, Matt and Collin, as you know by now, love sports. They play a game they call *knee football*, which—from what I can tell—involves rapidly trying to crawl past each other, breaking tackles, while carrying a pillow. They play it with a level of enthusiasm that causes the light in the ceiling below them to rattle.

In the family room, I always catch them throwing footballs at a pillow they've propped up on the sofa—which happens to be right in front of a window. Matt throws footballs so hard and fast that they resemble speeding bullets, so I keep warning the boys that they aren't allowed to throw balls in the house, and they're going to miss at some point and break the window.

For Christmas one of them got a new basketball. They decided to work on their passing skills even though their little sister was standing between them. I saw them and told them to stop and warned them that they were likely to hit her in the head.

"No way we'd do that. We don't miss," was the reply. Just as the sentence was uttered, BAM! Right in the nose. The look on their faces was one of absolute shock.

Now, of course, they didn't *intend* to do that. Still, any rational thinking individual would realize the possibility of non-NBA players messing up a pass was rather high. That, coupled with a four-year-old jumping up and down in between them, would have caused them to stop passing. They were sent off for a time-out as they continued assuring us it wasn't intentional and saying they were sorry.

I'm sure you are horrified by the idiocy of this story, but it's true and perfectly highlights the trouble with trusting teenage brains to function properly.

Some days I just look at our teenagers and think they must have dropped off an alien planet. It's not that they have three eyes or green skin; it's that they do the strangest things for seemingly no reason.

It turns out there *is* a reason! Brain researchers found the frontal lobe, which controls impulses and the ability to anticipate consequences and react accordingly, is undeveloped in teenagers. In fact, it doesn't fully develop until they're past college age. According to a research paper for the Coalition for Juvenile Justice, hard science demonstrates that teenagers are not fully mature in judgment, problem solving, and decision making. Our government realizes this truth, which is why twenty-one is the legal drinking age, and people can't vote or join the military until they are eighteen years old.

Brain and developmental research shows these facts: teenagers experience "reward-deficiency syndrome," which means they are no longer stimulated by activities that thrilled them as younger children, so they engage in riskier activities to achieve similar levels of excitement. Further, teens are forced to rely on the emotional center in the brain when making decisions because the frontal lobes aren't fully developed until they are about twenty-five years old.[1] Dealing with teens is a very different task from dealing with toddlers or younger children. Teens have bigger issues to deal with, which means you do too.

ILLUSIVE ACCOUNTABILITY

The temptation in our overanalyzed society is to blame everything but the problem. Experts continue to find new ways to define why the problems we have are out of our control and, thus, we need either therapy or drugs to deal with them. Take for example our nation's obesity problem. As shown elsewhere in the book, more than 63 percent of Americans are considered overweight. People now often blame genetics. Of course, that doesn't address why only now are we seeing the problem. Fifty years ago, half our population wasn't too fat. I guess that means genetics wasn't involved back then? Today my husband read a news report that claims obesity is caused by people catching a virus, which alters their stem cells. Okay . . . does anyone still believe it is caused by overeating and underexercising? No, because that means we're responsible and in charge of our destinies.

> *Discipline doesn't break a child's spirit half as often as the lack of it breaks a parent's heart.*
> —AUTHOR UNKNOWN

Nonpermissive parents accept that people should be held accountable for their actions. If your teens miss curfew, do they blame someone else for their tardiness? If they flunk a test because they didn't study, do they blame the teacher or other commitments for their lack of preparation? That is typical teen behavior. In fact, it is fairly typical adult behavior too. It's the type of society we've become. Instead of being accountable, we search for other reasons, reasons out of our control, for the choices we make.

Does this description of teenagers sound familiar to you? They . . .

- are stubborn
- test limits and push boundaries
- are easily annoyed
- lose their tempers
- argue with adults
- refuse to comply with rules and directions
- blame others for their mistakes
- deliberately annoy other people

Of course! It describes almost every teen at some point. How do you deal with it? I once read an article filled with advice from a child expert. She was on the board of numerous permissive-parent-friendly organizations. Her thesis was that children will behave in the way their parents assume they will. Therefore, if parents assume children will be honest or kind, they will be honest or kind. If given unconditional love, children will give unconditional love. So what happens when life doesn't work out that way? She basically counsels that parents should continue to think positively.

> *Man must cease attributing his problems to his environment and learn again to exercise his will—his personal responsibility.*
>
> —ALBERT EINSTEIN

You know, that sounds lovely to me. It also sounds like she might have named her baby Starchild, spent hours giving infant massages, and has a teenager who rules her house. Wake up! Nonpermissive parents accept the fact that, even though their teens know right from wrong, they still do wrong things sometimes and make mistakes. If not corrected and reminded why it's wrong, they will think the behavior is acceptable. I guarantee every parent will experience a less-than-respectful conversation when a child becomes a teenager, even if the parent has always treated the child with respect. It doesn't mean the child is a mutant. It means he needs maturing, and that's the parent's job. Nonpermissive parents tell their teens to control their anger, treat their parents with respect, follow rules, stop bugging their siblings, and own up to their mistakes.

In contrast, permissive parents never blame the children or hold them accountable for their actions. Rather, they blame circumstances or disorders if their children misbehave. There is even one disorder identified by the *Diagnostic and Statistical Manual of Mental Disorders* (DSM-IV), published by the American Psychiatric Association, called Oppositional Defiant Disorder (ODD). Every teen I know is both oppositional and defiant. It seems to be in their DNA at that point in their lives.

I don't want to make light of serious behavioral issues. Some teens' actions are so over-the-top that they are borderline dangerous to themselves and others. Those teens truly need full-time professional help. There should be no shame in getting therapy as it can be exactly what is needed in conjunction with effective parenting techniques. The problem is that many parents use their teen's "medical condition" as an excuse not to correct their own permissive parenting. The result is that small issues go unchecked, and the parents are shocked when the teen spins wildly out of control.

KIDS WHO ACT OUT

Instead of parenting teens who own up to their shortcomings and work on ways to better themselves, permissive parents with their blame-the-behavior, not-the-child theory are forced to find some other reason for their child not being able to follow rules and behave properly. I want to let you in on one of the least-talked-about behavioral secrets.

> *Obstinacy is will asserting itself without being able to justify itself. It is persistence without a reasonable motive. It is the tenacity of self-love substituted for that of reason and conscience.*
>
> —HENRI FREDERIC AMIEL

The son of one of my friends gained early acceptance into Yale. I congratulated her, and she said with a bit of disdain, "Yes, and he got in even though he took the Scholastic Aptitude Test (SAT) with a time limit," and added, "unlike many others." I had no idea what she was talking about. She explained—and I have since confirmed—that, at least on the East Coast, this is a very widespread practice. The SAT and American College Test (ACT) offer "challenged children" an *untimed* college entrance exam. All the child has to do is get a doctor to write a note saying the child has some kind of DSM-IV condition, such as attention deficit disorder (ADD), attention-deficit/hyperactivity disorder (ADHD), obsessive-compulsive disorder (OCD), or ODD. The list is pretty broad, and the note is seemingly easy to obtain. One doctor told me he wrote notes for every friend he knew who had a kid taking the college entrance exams.

Well, you would think schools would see that it was *untimed* and take that into consideration when comparing the scores to a child whose test was timed. Not so fast. The exam companies aren't allowed to disclose that a child's "disability" allowed him to take the test without a time limit.

I had Laurel take the ACT at fourteen years old because she wanted to get into a competitive math camp. Her score was extremely high, and by the time she needs to take the test for a college application, I'm sure she can come close to a perfect math score . . . if she doesn't have to worry about the time limit since most of her mistakes are due to rushing. Does she have a disorder? No, but I could easily find someone to write a note stating she does.

So in many cases, perfectly fine children get a huge advantage over other kids, the schools are none the wiser, and children learn they aren't held accountable for their own behaviors. Did they take a preparation test? Did they pay attention in school? Did they study enough? If the child is just *not* smart, even an untimed test won't make a difference, but in the highly competitive college world, where a few points one way or the other can make a huge impact, an untimed test is a great advantage.

You might wonder why the colleges haven't caught on. They are well aware of what goes on. To some, gaming the system is a creative, out-of-the-box approach. Plus, it fits nicely into the theories held by permissive child development experts, many of whom teach at the highest-rated universities.

TEEN TRIALS . . . AND ERRORS

Back to basic teenage behavior. Like every other teen in history, yours will likely go through a period of being defiant, cantankerous, obstinate, and sometimes (you suspect) deaf and mute since they don't seem to hear a word you say and rarely reply with more than a grunt. What should you do? Permissive-parenting

Web sites tell you what you shouldn't do. They often say that punishing teens does little to teach children about their mistakes, and the same holds true for lecturing. Most of us probably remember being lectured when we were young, and if we are honest, would readily admit that we dreaded it.

> *Obstinacy is the result of the will*
> *forcing itself into the place of the intellect.*
> —ARTHUR SCHOPENHAUER

So I guess that means, if kids dread punishment, we should not use it? *Cuckoo, cuckoo.* Is anyone home? This is the kind of malarkey dished out nonstop by the permissive-parenting movement. What is the result? I ran across a parenting Web site that welcomed readers to submit parenting questions. One woman wrote that her teenage daughter, an only child, was disrespectful and argumentative. In response, she is grounded, but the mother then explains that her daughter is frequently able to talk her out of enforcing the punishment. When her daughter brought home low grades, the mother cut out her after-school sports. Not surprisingly, the daughter had a snit fit and announced she'd quit sports altogether. She morphed the complaint into a diatribe about how she didn't have all name-brand clothing and that the mother didn't do enough for her.

The correct response to this kind of teenage reasoning is to reply that you'll discuss it all at a later date. But this mom fell into the guilt trap. She was having panic attacks and sleepless nights. Why? She feared that if she followed through on punishments, her daughter might not like her or respect her.

STAYING ON TRACK WITH TEENS

It's obvious the problem is with the parent's behavior; the teen is normal. The daughter is questioning, pushing the limits, arguing, and forming her identity. This is one of the points where the parent needs to step in and weed out bad, destructive, or simply obnoxious behavior and explain why the child should not behave in that manner.

> *I used to be indecisive, but now I'm not sure.*
>
> —TOMMY COOPER

Look at it from the teen's perspective. Why should she bother to earn good grades or be respectful since her mother won't follow through on any consequence? When her mother cuts out after-school sports, she immediately begins to obsess about how this will impact her daughter. It's a temporary ban on after-school sports. It's highly unlikely the girl will decide to morph into a couch potato in a week. Her mother is clearly a permissive parent, who is more focused on having her child like *her* than she is with raising a child whom *anyone else* might like. Her daughter realizes her mother is a pushover and then tries to imply that her poor grades, rude and inconsiderate treatment of her mother, and every other issue in her life will be solved by her mother buying her name-brand clothes. It's the height of idiocy for the mother to expect that her child will respect her at all. There's a simple reason her daughter walks over her like a doormat. It's because the mother lets her do it.

So how are permissive parents coached to handle this? Here was part of the answer. In a nutshell the mother was counseled to let her child continue with the after-school sports, since so many other children don't take part in enough sports.

Huh? What do they have to do with this woman and her daughter?

> *Against logic there is no armor like ignorance.*
>
> —DR. LAURENCE J. PETER

Let me see if I have their logic right. Because some kids are sedentary, we should never keep them from an outdoor activity, especially if it would mean they would have time to reflect on missing the activity and thinking about what behavior led to their punishment. Instead of parenting them, they suggest unconditional support and encouragement. Encouragement of what? Getting bad grades? Arguing with their mother? Complaining that they should have designer clothes? I wouldn't think any of that behavior should be encouraged. But I'm not an "adolescent development expert." I'm just a mom, but a nonpermissive mom, and I know that those experts haven't raised children I'd want to be around. Society does not like rude, whiny, complaining underachievers who think the world owes them something. They are the people we all avoid.

STRUCTURE AND CONSEQUENCES

Teens need structure and solid parenting, instead of a free rein with no consequences. Here are some important points:

1. *Listen to your teen.* Often, we're so busy with our own lives that we simply don't make time to talk. Sometimes they will have valid points that you need to understand. Once they realize you do understand the entire issue, they are more likely to abide by your rules or suggestions.

2. *Be consistent.* Parents who wonder why a child behaves a certain way eventually realize the problem is really with them because they are unable to be consistent in a child's punishment. Focus on big issues that impact a child's health or opportunities. While I think the way children physically appear (with no nose studs, for instance) is important, I don't think a messy room will keep them from being all they can be.

3. *Pick the important battles.* One trick I use is to say no to something that I really don't mind that much and let them present the reasons why they should be able to do it. Then I say that they've presented good reasons why I should change my mind,

and I do. They get to win on an issue, and it role models the process of rational discussions. Teens learn they can get what they want through discussion instead of yelling.

4. *Pass on morals and ethics.* Think about it. If your children don't learn from you, they will pick up lessons elsewhere. Almost any television show they watch will teach that lying, cheating, and stealing are acceptable means to achieve the desired results. They will learn that it's acceptable to risk their safety for sixty seconds of fame. If your children get kicked out of school for cheating but grew up seeing you cheat on your taxes or in your golf game, why should they feel cheating is bad? During their childhood, you set the foundation for the values they will display as adults. While consistently talking about moral and ethical choices with our children, it was wonderful when they became involved in our church youth group. The young adults who lead the group upheld the same principles we did. They were in a setting with peers where they could discuss and form opinions about ethical and moral behavior that further reinforced the lessons we were teaching them at home.

5. *Resist the urge to want to be your children's friend.* They have friends. They need a parent. I read an article in *USA Today* about research done by Synovate, a market research firm. It surveyed one thousand parents with these results:

- 43 percent want to be their children's best friends
- 40 percent would buy their children everything they wanted if they could

---

It is . . . sometimes easier to head an institute for the study of child guidance than it is to turn one brat into a decent human being.

—JOSEPH WOOD KRUTCH

Ian Pierpoint, a senior vice president for the firm, reported that one mother told him she didn't make her child do his homework because it would make him unhappy. While you might assume kids would think that was great, one twenty-two-year-old to whom Pierpoint spoke said, "There's no way I'm going to be like my mom. My mom does everything for me. She's made me lazy. There is no way kids are going to rule my house."[2] Nonpermissive parents love their children, but they have rules and consequences for their children breaking those rules. Be consistent. As Francis Bacon said, "Look to make your course regular, that men may know beforehand what they may expect."

HANDS ON OR HANDS OFF?

What should you do when your teen refuses to come home on time? How do you know which issues to address? You monitor your children. Yes, you can call it *spying*. Permissive parents get wide-eyed at the thought of *invading* their children's privacy. "Why, my children might think I don't trust them," they protest. Bingo. Trust is earned, not given. Further, the trust earned as a young child cannot be transferred to the alien years. Nonpermissive parents understand that teens need space, not absolute freedom. While I hate to sound like a lawyer, a behavior contract is a terrific idea.

Research indicates teens living in a household with rules that are enforced turn out better. The National Center on Addiction and Substance Abuse (CASA) at Columbia University, in its sixth annual national teen substance abuse survey, found that parents who are "hands on" have children who smoke less, drink less, and use drugs less. These parents have established a culture in their homes that revolves around basic rules and expectations. The report finds, "Contrary to conventional wisdom, teens in 'hands-on' households are more likely to have an excellent relationship with their parents than teens with 'hands-off' parents." Equally important was the conclusion that adults should be parents to their children, not pals.[3]

MONITORING REALITY

I want to know what my children are up to, who they are spending time with, and what they are doing during that time. You can ask your teen for the answers, but during the alien years they may not tell the truth, the whole truth, and nothing but the truth. They may not be lying; rather, they conveniently leave things out—things of which you might not approve. I don't know a parent who has time to follow his children 24/7, nor would I recommend it. That is a controlling parent. A nonpermissive parent lays out the boundaries, allows the teens to freely move about, and then monitors their progress. You may be one of the fortunate few, and every time you check on your teens, they are doing exactly what you expect of them. Wonderful. That's not my reality, and it's not what most parents face. How do I know? I monitor.

> *Nobody's family can hang out the sign, "Nothing the matter here."*
>
> —CHINESE PROVERB

I had a friend who frequently told me how wonderful her thirteen-year-old daughter was. She never, ever had a problem with her. The girl made good grades, she was active in sports, and she had many friends. But she had a few more friends Mom didn't know about. Here's the reality: when you boast about how perfect your child is in every way, you are virtually asking for someone to burst your bubble.

And that's what happened. Her daughter asked to go to the movies with friends one evening. Since Mom knew and liked her daughter's friends, she let her go. It turned out she was meeting friends Mom didn't know about . . . *friends* from another town. *Friends* who seemed quite a bit older than this girl, wore baggy pants and baseball caps sideways on their heads, and used language best suited for R-rated movies. *Friends* who had no intention of going to the movies with her.

> *Nothing in the world is more dangerous than sincere ignorance and conscientious stupidity.*
>
> —MARTIN LUTHER KING JR.

I got a phone call from a mutual friend of this mother and me. She had just driven down the main street in town and saw this girl in the alley next to the movie theater, deep in a make-out session with a boy she was positive her mother didn't know. A group of equally undesirable looking boys was surrounding them. My friend wanted to know what I thought she should do. This would crush the mother's vision of her perfect daughter, but this woman was genuinely concerned for the girl's safety at that very moment. She didn't want to hurt her friendship with the mother, but she couldn't live with herself if something happened to the girl. I told her to call the mother right away. I knew she would be furious because her daughter wasn't what she expected and be embarrassed after all the boasting she'd done, but I said the embarrassment would be compounded if our friend was kept in the dark and even more people passed by, recognized her, and saw what was going on. More importantly, the girl could very easily get into a dangerous situation.

Kids make mistakes. Maybe this was the first time she'd done this; maybe it wasn't. It was certainly time for her mother to get a reality check. It doesn't mean her daughter is a bad child, it simply means she had not been monitoring her daughter well enough to know that a problem was developing. I have faced and continue to be challenged *frequently* by my own children's shortcomings. This isn't a book that will tell you how to keep your children from making mistakes. Mistakes, even big ones, can be invaluable tools of learning. The best you can do is stay involved and love your children, realizing they (like you and everyone else) are fallible.

> *A child today faces more sexual signals and temptations on the way to school than his grandfather did on Saturday night when he was looking for them.*[4]
>
> —SEAN MCDOWELL

So how do you find out what the reality is in your teenagers' lives? Know their friends and their habits.

1. *Check the "called" list on their cell phone, and write down the numbers.* If there are some you don't recognize, ask who they are. Do this a couple of times before telling your teen you're doing it. What happens once they do realize what you're doing is that they then delete the list right after each phone call.

   My story: Laurel was very tired each morning to the point that two teachers mentioned it to me. Laurel told them her little sister was waking her up in the middle of the night, and she had a hard time getting back to sleep. One of the teachers indicated she personally thought it was cruel and unusual punishment to force children to room together. When Laurel came home, I told her I would move her sister into another sibling's room, and she begged me not to. I figured out that being woken up by her sister wasn't the issue; so what would keep her from getting enough sleep? She didn't have a computer or laptop in her room, but she did have her cell phone, which she also used as an alarm clock. I took it and saw that she was phoning people and getting calls from people until two in the morning. That's why she wasn't getting enough sleep. Her little sister was likely waking up because of all the chatter. I wrote down all the numbers and checked the faces and names attached to them in the phone contact list. I asked her about the ones I didn't know. I made the rule that she had to turn in her cell phone at 9:00 P.M. She protested, using the excuse that she needed it as her alarm clock. I gave her my alarm clock. She frowned.

The more things a man is ashamed of,
the more respectable he is.

—GEORGE BERNARD SHAW

2. *Check their networking sites, such as Facebok, MySpace, AIM buddy
    lists, and the like.* You will likely be really surprised by what you
    find on your children's pages and on the pages of their friends.
    I went to the page for one of Laurel's girlfriends, and this sweet
    girl had a Web page with risqué pictures and writings filled with
    foul language. I couldn't believe it was really this girl's page. I'm
    positive her parents had no idea. Well, it certainly changed my
    impression of her and meant I was extra vigilant whenever Laurel
    was around her.

    Last night I checked Laurel's AIM page, and she had an
    "away" message that, while not dirty, was certainly not whole-
    some, *and* she had listed her cell phone number. Keep in mind
    this is a very intelligent teenager, but it seems teens often leave
    common sense in their lockers at school. I e-mailed her to replace
    the "away" message with something more appropriate and to take
    her cell phone number off. I explained that any friend of hers
    would already know her number or know who to call to get it. If
    kids leave their computers on or write down their friends' infor-
    mation, other people can access those pages too. I explained that
    if they called her on her cell phone, she'd assume she knew them,
    which could be dangerous. Always explain to your teens that you
    take actions to ensure their safety and help guide them on a path
    that will give them the best options for their lives.

    Yes, you've figured out that your children can simply set up
    accounts you don't know about. Here's what you do: set up your
    own account on these sites. Use your children's names and nick-
    names to do searches on the site. Ask their siblings what sites
    they're on. If you find they're creating accounts without your
    knowledge, you may not be able to stop them since they can
    access computers everywhere, but you do know that it likely isn't
    the only area of their lives where they are disobeying rules. Turn
    around the trust argument, and tell them it's tougher to trust
    them if they do this. The other benefit is that you will find out
    how much time your teens spend on the computer. One boy,

instant messaging Laurel, had been online for thirteen hours and forty minutes! No wonder kids are sedentary.

> *The greatest minds are capable of the greatest*
> *vices as well as the greatest virtues.*
>
> —RENE DESCARTES

3.   *Check their school lockers.* Being the student body president, head cheerleader, or future valedictorian does not make them immune from making stupid mistakes, such as using drugs or alcohol or hiding harmful habits from you. If your children attend a permissive school, the administration will certainly frown upon your conducting your own locker check, as will many of the parents.

   I was in the hallway, checking Matt's locker one day while he was in class. A mother, a friend of mine, came up and asked what I was doing. She was aghast when I explained. I heard the phrase I've come to expect: "He'll think you don't trust him. He'll be embarrassed if the other kids see you're checking his locker."

   I replied, "I don't care. If there is nothing to hide, there will be nothing to find, and eventually I won't need to check his locker. He will have earned my trust."

   Permissive parents seriously believe it's better to let their children take drugs in front of friends instead of letting them be embarrassed in front of friends. Frankly, if more parents checked lockers, there wouldn't be drugs and alcohol in school, and we could all stop!

> *It is good to be without vices, but it*
> *is not good to be without temptations.*
>
> —WALTER BAGEHOT

4. *Check their backpacks and/or purses and their bedroom drawers and closets.* If your children are teenagers, they will have numerous temptations thrown at them. That's the reality. Permissive parents ignore the pitfalls. Nonpermissive parents point them out to their children and help them avoid the temptations. They also find out if their children have tripped up and help them correct the problems.

    Laurel protested that I was invading her privacy when I came into her room one day and told her I was going to check her purse. I agreed, which shocked her. Then I told her because I realized it was unfair, I would let her check my purse and go through my bedroom drawers.

    She said, "I don't want to. There isn't anything interesting."

    I replied, "But you're still free to do it, and if I don't find interesting things in your drawers and purse, I may eventually stop looking because you will have earned my trust."

    Yes, your children could find hiding places somewhere else, but at least you're making it more difficult for them to hide harmful items, and they will realize you care about what they do. Repeat to yourself that nonpermissive parents care and love their children enough to do what it takes to help them stay out of trouble or catch them quickly when they fall into it so they can be helped.

> *You are in control of your life. Don't ever forget that.*
> *You are what you are because of the conscious*
> *and subconscious choices you have made.*
>
> —BARBARA HALL

5. *Volunteer to be the team parent or drive their sports teams to events.* There are numerous benefits. Each season I volunteer for one

of the children's teams. Because we have a large van (to transport our family) I also drive part of the team to away games. The really nice part of this is that you get to spend time with your children while they're taking part in something they usually love. You can share in their joy and be there to cheer them on. It facilitates closeness in your relationship.

Next, I find that for the first two minutes the kids think about a parent overhearing what they are talking about. After that they forget you're there. My, oh my, what your ears will hear! The children talk about their classmates and who is doing what with whom. They discuss teachers, assignments, and grades. Kids who haven't done well (sometimes including your own) get razzed by the others. Just sit quietly and listen. Knowledge is power.

> *Regard your good name as the richest jewel you can possibly be possessed of, for credit is like fire; when once you have kindled it you may easily preserve it, but if you once extinguish it, you will find it an arduous task to rekindle it again.*
>
> —SOCRATES

So you are a vigilant, nonpermissive parent, and your child still goes off track. It's not the end of the world. Been there, done that. Permissive parents never face that though, because nothing is off-limits except sometimes drugs. Even then, permissive parents adopt the attitude that this, too, shall pass, so let me just get on with my life. Nonpermissive parents pay attention. We try our best, but we are fallible, and so are our children. The key is that you catch on that something is amiss, and you can hopefully stop it before your children permanently hurt themselves or their future opportunities.

I'm not a lawyer and don't intend to become one, but again, a contract might be helpful. When you can turn to a written contract signed by you and your teen, it makes it a lot tougher for him to argue that you aren't being fair. *Fair* is the four-letter word teens seem to use the most at this point. For a sample contract, please refer to appendix A in the back of this book.

WHAT WORKS, WHAT DOESN'T

In my experience, one consequence that simply doesn't work for teens is spanking. I remember thinking that I would much rather get a spanking as punishment and get it over with than to miss a dance, a party, or a movie night. Today there's a whole new array of privileges to lose. Consider taking their iPod, Wii, or whatever the latest gizmo is. That is real punishment for a teen! Read on.

From R. J. in Missouri:

I am the father of three teens. Two attend college and my youngest is a sophomore in high school. I found that as kids age you need to find a different kind of punishment. When our children did something that deserved punishment, we made them write a paper, single spaced, that described the problem, offered potential reasonable solutions, and at least two Bible verses that related. One of my regrets is that I didn't keep these papers. They must have collectively written several dozen. But my two oldest are majoring in journalism now, and I would like to think that my punishment had something to do with their excellent writing abilities. My middle child is considering a minor in theology. Go figure!

From A. N. in Kentucky:

I'm a school teacher, and I know that there are few children who enjoy writing English papers. But you know the saying, "Practice makes perfect!" When my daughter misbehaves, I make her write a paper describing her behavior and how she can change it.

TOUGH LOVE WORKS

Divorce is difficult for children of all ages, as is learning how to function in a new, combined family, if one of your parents remarries. Sometimes teens have a very difficult time dealing with the changes in their lives. They don't know how to act, they question what their role is, even whether their parents love them, and so they simply act out.

> *There are times that parenthood seems nothing more than feeding the hand that bites you.*
>
> —PETER DE VRIES

We've certainly had our issues over the years after combining my three children with Joe's three children. He had a nine-year-old daughter, I had a seven-year-old daughter, we both had six-year-old sons, and we both had three-year-old sons. The boys all got along great. Two were friends before we even met, and all are now best friends as well as brothers. Off the top of my head, I can't think of a single fight they've had. They occasionally complain about each other, but I don't think they've ever had a major disagreement.

Not so with the girls. Each was the oldest child. Each was the "princess" in the family. Neither wanted to share the throne. They fought for a while and then just decided to ignore each other.

Then we had another child, a girl. Sumner is an adorable little girl now, but she was one heck of an unattractive baby. We even joked about it a bit. The girls didn't mind that. But one day, Joe looked at Sumner and realized she was changing. He called out to me, "Look, she is really becoming beautiful!" Jordan, who was thirteen years old at the time, happened to be in the room and left immediately.

Thirteen is a rough age. She was rebelling quite a bit and didn't like the fact that we had strict rules at our house. Earlier that day we had caught her trying to throw new clothes into the outside garbage can. They were appropriate clothes, meaning she didn't want anything to do with them. One weekend night was reserved for a family dinner at a restaurant. She would sulk through the meal because she wanted to be out with friends. She wanted to listen to CDs with lyrics of which we didn't approve. The musicians swore, degraded women, and used racist language. We didn't allow anyone to watch MTV for basically the same reasons. She complained she didn't have the same rules at her mom's house, and sometimes she simply would stay there even on our weekends. The clothing incident followed by Joe's comments about Sumner just did something that sent her over the edge.

The next morning I was leaving work (I was lucky enough to be able to take the infants to the office with me) and glanced down at the top of Sumner's head. The hair was missing. Yes, an entire one-inch-large circle of hair had simply been cut off to the scalp. As my mind raced back through time, I remembered that about five minutes after Joe's comment, Jordan came back to the room and then took Sumner with her to the bedroom to play. Apparently to play beauty parlor! Sure enough, when I got home and went into her bathroom, I found the scissors and the hair right there on the counter. She couldn't explain why she had done it. It was completely irrational, but it was also dangerously over the line.

We refused to let Jordan come back to the house for three months and then said the only way she could return was if she really wanted to live with the rules of our household. For a month she was fine and probably happy not to have to come over. But even teens, no matter how much they rebel, want structure. Always explain that you are punishing them because you care about them and want them to learn a lesson that will help them to become terrific adults. I even explain to the kids that it would be much easier for me to simply ignore it and let them do whatever they want. That's what parents do when they don't care about their children. Make sure your kids know that giving in to them, meeting their wishes, never punishing them, and simply letting them do what they want is the easy way out for a parent. Those are not parents who love their children. They are parents who don't love their children enough to take the time to raise them. If your children hear this explanation often enough, it will eventually sink in. Anyway, by the end of the third month, Jordan was begging to come back. She missed being around the other kids and realized she liked being part of the family, even with the rules. She's been a different child and has blossomed into a wonderful and loving young adult since then. Sumner adores her.

> *Most people do not really want freedom, because freedom involves responsibility, and most people are frightened of responsibility.*
>
> —SIGMUND FREUD

In the end, structure and safety will always appeal to teenagers more than permissive parenting by moms and/or dads who will do anything and allow any behavior just so they can be their children's *friends*. I have a friend who told me she was her daughter's best friend. A lot of parents say that and wish it were true. Why? What are you thinking? Your children are weird if they want a person at least twenty years older than they are as a best friend. I hold my tongue, but I'm dying to say, "Your child has a best friend, but it's not you, no matter what you do or what you think." You may be great friends with your parents in your adult years, but teens with parents desperate to be *best friends* can get away with murder. "Don't you trust me? I thought we were friends" is a frequent statement. "You don't go through your friend's purse or backpack, do you?"

Permissive parents get even worse when there is divorce involved. They fully believe that the fewer rules kids have, the more they'll want to be with that parent. That may be true for a while but not for very long. I call it the *Disney Dad Syndrome*, but it's the same with some mothers too. Life at their house is always fun and games. There are no consequences for bad behavior. The children are perfect, no matter what they do or don't do. Have you ever been to Disney World? After a certain amount of time there, you're dying to get away. You're sick of the snack food, tired of the noise and bedlam, and simply want to be someplace calm and reassuring. Make sure your children understand that you have rules because you care about them.

From J. T in California:

We found out that our teenage son, who otherwise was a well-behaved boy, had gone to some pornography Internet sites and had even been into porn chat rooms. He was in high school, but we sat him down and asked him if he still wanted to live at home. If so, we told him, this would not be tolerated because it was wrong. He said okay, and we followed up with some counseling for him. That was the end of it. Our philosophy is that if one of the children doesn't want to live by the house rules, then he is free to move out. He can always stay home or come back if he agrees to follow the rules.

I read an article about a mom in Grand Rapids, Michigan, who came up with a great punishment for her fifteen-year-old son who was suspended from school. She says, "If I had said to him, 'Travis, no TV for three days,' who cares about that? He would have forgotten it. When you come up with creative things, kids really remember." So what did she do? She made her son spend the suspension day picking up trash on a busy street, wearing a sign stating, "I made a bad choice in school, now I'm living with it."

When my son J. D. read this, he thought it was a great punishment. He said there was no way he'd do something if it meant punishment that was really embarrassing.

R-E-S-P-E-C-T

Rodney Dangerfield is famous for saying, "I get no respect." And I hear many permissive parents saying the same thing these days. But in my opinion, it's their own fault.

Another newspaper I read detailed an incident that happened with a seventh-grade girl who was suspended for a week after bullying another student. Then her mom got involved, and things got a lot worse for Miasha. Her mother made Miasha stand outside a different school each day wearing a poster, reading, "I engaged in bullying behavior. I got suspended from school. Don't be like me. Stop bullying." Why did her mom do it? She says, "I don't want that kind of environment at the school my child attends or the school any child attends."

These mothers don't want to ridicule their children. They would prefer not to embarrass them. But they realize that, if these kids don't learn the lesson at this age, they will soon be on the path to making poor decisions they'll be living with for life. These moms love their children enough to parent them. It's true that maturing teens are frequently frustrated by structure (although that doesn't mean they don't need it). Due to their changing bodies, their emotions often go haywire.

At this very moment, for instance, one of our big boys, Matt, is sitting in his room. We are on vacation, and the rest of the family has gone biking and to the beach for the day. Why is he here? Because while I was talking to him about how to handle arguments with his sister, he got so mad at me that he swore at me. Big, impressive cuss words. So big they earned him a full day in his room to think about alternate language that could have been used. Of course, I would prefer that he go out and have fun with the rest of the family. But his circumstances are due entirely to his behavior and choices. Next time he is tempted to resort to swearing, he will think about the repercussions of his actions and, hopefully, make a better choice. We have four teenagers, and it is very rare (although not unheard-of) for them to utter a cuss word. That's because we are nonpermissive parents.

> *Respect for one's parents is the highest duty of civil life.*
> —CHINESE PROVERB

Expecting your children to behave in ways that are respectful to those around them is not unreasonable. When permissive parents say there is no way to stop them, what they are really saying is that they are not willing to enforce the punishment that will result in a change in their children's behavior. As soon as you lift the punishment, they may go right back to the same disrespectful behavior, meaning you have to punish them again. But kids aren't dumb; they don't enjoy punishment. Pretty soon they'll behave in the right way. Hopefully, by the time they move on and move out, they'll choose to behave respectfully on their own. There is no excuse for a parent to stop trying simply because it is a tough job.

Requiring children to show respect and follow the rules at home is the only way to survive the alien years and help kids grow into mature, responsible adults.

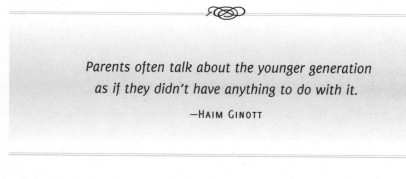

Parents often talk about the younger generation
as if they didn't have anything to do with it.
—HAIM GINOTT

Driving, Dating, and Other Death-Defying Feats

*It is amazing how quickly the kids learn to drive
a car, yet are unable to understand the
lawnmower, snow blower, or vacuum cleaner.*

—Ben Bergor

Panic! That's what we did when we realized that our child (who can't find her retainer in the morning even though it's in her mouth) will be the intellectual force commanding a three-thousand-pound driving machine! Somewhere, somehow, the little girl we used to strap into the car seat turned into the young woman in the driver's seat. How did that happen?

Honestly, we tried to forget about it. We knew she was taking her driver's education classes, but we decided to pretend it was theoretical instruction rather than practical, which she might actually be tempted to put to use. When she came home to talk about what she was learning, we quickly changed the subject. It didn't stop the inevitable. When we realized that she had her heart set on doing the same thing every other teen her age was doing, we tried what we thought was a surefire winner.

"Great! Get your license," we said and quickly followed that with, "but you'll need to buy your own car." We knew she only had $312 saved, and we had always been very explicit with the children that they would have to pay for their own cars.

My parents actually offered to *give* me a car—a car they knew I wouldn't want to drive for fear someone, anyone I knew, might see me. It was a beauty—a 1961 Cadillac Sedan De Ville in all its white leather interior, enormous pointy-tail-finned glory! I know that back in *their* day it must have been quite a looker, but that day was far removed from today. In my present-day view, the car was the largest monstrosity cruising the streets, impossible to miss. Anyone driving it must have had an I-want-to-be-labeled-a-geek-forever fetish. There was simply *no way* to drive that car with any sense of dignity. My parents, of course, didn't see it that way. At least I don't think they did. Anyway, what they told me was that they wanted me to have a car I would be safe in if, God forbid, I were in a wreck. This, they said, was a solid, well-built American car, despite its age.

I had come to a crossroads in my life: I could sit at home, calling friends to see if they would give me a ride to where I wanted to go, or I could cast any aspirations of popularity aside and climb behind the wheel. I turned to my parents and said, "Gee, thanks."

To this day, despite their valid safety points, I have a sneaking suspicion they were snickering the first time I pulled out of the driveway. Don't you know they were right about everything? Within an hour I had accidentally run a stop sign and stopped mere inches before hitting another car although, even if I had hit the other car, I would have been perfectly cocooned in the . . . And that's the part that to this day drives me nuts. My parents' car choice kept me safe. Eventually, my parents gave that car away (clearly no one would buy it), I think to one of those tax donation charities that promises to give you a large, written, tax-deductible estimate for any car they can push, pull, or drive away.

By that point I think they mistakenly thought I had made enough mistakes and, hopefully, learned from them that I had perfected my driving technique. So they let me drive my dad's adorable VW bug convertible. My parents quickly regretted that decision. Following the next football game, my fellow cheerleaders and I stuffed our Texas-sized maroon-and-gold pom-poms into the trunk of the car. Of course, on a VW the trunk is in the front end. We lived up to the cheerleader reputation for intelligence, because when we closed the hood, it didn't shut completely. We didn't notice that a pom-pom was stuck in the latch. As I blissfully cruised along Highway 290 from Dripping Springs to Oak Hill, Texas, so we could get pizza at Mr. Gatti's, the trunk blew open, cracking the windshield. I was stuck bumming rides for quite a while.

I always look for the positive lessons that can come from a bad experience, and this next one has certainly made me a much more aware driver. It was early in the morning. Of course, anything before noon seemed early before I had kids! Anyway, I needed a cup of coffee and pulled into a 7-11. Bleary-eyed, I walked in, poured a cup, paid, and headed back out to the car. While clutching the all-important liquid adrenaline with one hand, I cranked the radio, put the car in reverse, and began backing up, ignoring the seemingly possessed men at the curb, making weird facial and hand gestures. *Slam!*

You know how things move in slow motion? I saw the coffee cup lift off into the air like an aerodynamically challenged spaceship, which quite quickly gave up the fight against the forces of gravity and plummeted right down into my lap. I'd been in such a rush to get to the coffee that I hadn't paid attention to the fact that I had wedged my car into a "kind of" parking spot. You know the type I'm talking about—it's not *quite* a spot, but you rationalize to yourself that it really *should* be. The problem is that the designer of this parking configuration, who must have a much higher level of public parking safety experience than I, had failed to take people like me into consideration. They assumed that erecting a light pole where there could have been a parking space would deter a clear-thinking individual from parking there. However, at that point in my life I was not a clear-thinking individual. And those possessed men? They just sat there holding their stomachs and laughing. *Women drivers!* I know that's what they were thinking!

Women must pay for everything. They do get more glory than men for comparable feats, but they also get more notoriety when they crash.

—AMELIA EARHART

The point is that I've been there. I've lived it. I can totally relate to a teenage driver, especially a female driver. Every thought is about boys, parties, and how soon you need to start cramming for the next test, instead of checking the rearview mirror, using the turn signals, and never stuffing your pom-poms in the trunk without double checking that it is securely closed. So when our daughter Jordan assured us that she had paid attention in class, was absolutely trustworthy, and would never have a wreck, we knew better.

"If you want to drive, you have to buy your own car," we said, assuming that would take care of the problem. The last thing we thought was that her mother would give her a car to drive (such are the issues of the modern blended family). It wasn't, however, as bad as we had expected. She started with her learner's permit, which allowed her to drive but only with a licensed driver who'd been driving for at least four years. After 120 days she was able to apply to take the driver's license exam. During the first three months of driving, she was only able to drive with a parent or adult. Over the next three months she could only transport family members, and not between midnight and 5:00 A.M. Good thing because she soon had what I'll call an "unfortunate encounter."

> *Another way to solve the traffic problems of this country is to pass a law that only paid-for cars be allowed to use the highways.*
> —WILL ROGERS

Jordan was driving out of Starbucks early one morning before an exam. (Starbucks provides the nutritional elements necessary for a teenage brain to function at test time.) Oops! She forgot to check for oncoming cars. Because of that, she had a not-so-friendly encounter with a pick-up truck and the lawnmower attached to it! Well, this being America, the other driver was an unlicensed, uninsured, illegal immigrant. In this case, that was good news. Why? He wanted nothing to do with a police report or anything else.

Our daughter said, "But what about the taillight that I knocked off the back of your truck?"

Oh that? Not to worry, he said. He didn't really need it. He just wanted to continue on his way to whatever off-the-books gardening job he was working. The lovely, relatively new, silver Subaru station wagon now had an artistic swath of red paint marking it from front to back! Her mom then banned her from driving for two months. She leaves for college next year, and we don't think her mom will let her take the car. She still doesn't have enough money saved to buy her own car, so we expect her to become well-known by the public transportation drivers. We will rest easier at night!

WOMEN DRIVERS

> I received a funny kids-and-driving email, which illustrates
> that all female drivers seem to be alike! A tree never
> hits an automobile except in self-defense.
>
> —AUTHOR UNKNOWN

From C. M. in Iowa:

Mischief runs in our family. Before our daughter had her driver's license, she decided she should take a driving lesson while we were running errands. We weren't gone long and didn't notice anything amiss when we got back. In fact, it wasn't until my husband was doing some yard work that he realized something was wrong. He noticed black electrical tape around one of the young maple trees. Our daughter had sideswiped the tree and bandaged it up, hoping we would not notice. She became a nurse, and tape is still part of her life!

We've all had driving accidents or made mistakes while on the road. But Joe and I reasoned it might be good parenting to simply remove the opportunity to make those mistakes. Why did she really need to drive anyway? At that point, we were also telling each other that she really didn't need to date until she was thirty either . . .

THE FRIGHTENING FACTS

We are not hypochondriacs. The teen fatality numbers are astounding, and it's a good idea to share them with kids as we did. They paint a sobering picture.

LEADING CAUSES OF DEATH AMONG TEENAGERS BY GENDER, 2004			
Cause of death	**Male**	**Female**	**Total**
Motor vehicles	3,662	1,967	5,629
Homicide	1,727	337	2,064
Suicide	1,481	435	1,916

Source: The Insurance Institute for Highway Safety[1]

> *It takes 8,460 bolts to assemble an automobile,*
> *and one nut to scatter it all over the road.*
>
> —AUTHOR UNKNOWN

Fortunately, as highway safety has increased, all traffic deaths, including teens, have decreased.[2]

The next issue you face is when your teen wants to ride as a passenger in someone else's car. Sixty-one percent of teenage passenger deaths in 2005 occurred in vehicles driven by another teenager. Among deaths of passengers of all ages, 19 percent occurred when a teenager was driving.[3]

PRIVILEGE AND RESPONSIBILITY

I imagine you are sufficiently scared senseless by these statistics. I was. It's at this point that you realize that death and taxes are not the only sure things in life. At a certain age, children become eligible to get their driver's licenses.

> *The best way to keep children at home*
> *is to make the home atmosphere pleasant—*
> *and let the air out of their tires.*
>
> —SAM LEVENSON

From M. P. in Connecticut:

My son needed to drive when he got his license because he was the school president and had meetings and school-related obligations that required him to get places. Because we have another child and live about eighteen minutes from the school, it made sense for all of us for him to be able to drive himself. Before we let him drive, we established a driving contract between us and our son. I downloaded the contract from the Internet, made him initial each section, and then sign in full. The car is a big privilege as it represents independence and freedom. If that gets taken away, kids are not happy! My son spent so much time involved with school and studying that he was unable to hold down a job. His grades were so good that he got into an Ivy League college, so in part—as a reward for his hard work—we bought the car for him. I had to work a job as well as my husband so that we could afford to finance the car, and we felt it was important for him to understand that everyone had to make sacrifices for him to have it.

There are numerous places to find guidelines for a teen driving contract, but I found one that is so thorough and well written that I think it's tough to beat. It's included as appendix B in the back of this book, along with notes about how to make the most of the contract with your teens. You can either use this one with your teen or go to the Web site to print one out. It's from www.parentingteendrivers.com. The Web site is free and run by Dale Wisely, who kindly offered to let me reprint it. Dale is a clinical psychologist who practiced child and adolescent psychology and heads the student services department of a public school system. He knows kids!

CREATIVE MONITORING

I like the idea of a contract, but Les Ladd in Highland, Michigan, also has a novel idea that I read about in a *Wall Street Journal* report. When his daughter, Sara, got her driver's license, he made her put a bumper sticker on her car. It asks, "How's My Teen Driving?" and has a toll-free number for people to call in their reports. Sara, reportedly, was mortified, but like most teens she was also desperate enough for a car that she was willing to do it. Mr. Ladd is apparently trying to make a business of the bumper sticker idea but found that other parents weren't as willing to publicly mark their child and invite criticism from strangers. What is wrong with strangers criticizing your children? I'm not talking about busybody critiques, such as "Hello, Mrs. Hill. While driving next to your daughter, I happened to notice that she didn't have her hands at the ten o'clock and two o'clock positions on the driver's wheel," but helpful, constructive ones, such as "Mrs. Hill your daughter was driving 75 miles an hour down Main Street while applying mascara and talking on her cell phone."

> *When buying a used car, punch the buttons*
> *on the radio. If all the stations are rock and roll,*
> *there's a good chance the transmission is shot.*
>
> —LARRY LUJACK

One of my friends didn't trust others to tell her how her son was driving. She would follow him without his knowing it. She would ask him what his plans were, who he was picking up, and where he was going. Next, she would park somewhere she knew he would drive by, and she'd wait for him to pass. Then she'd follow a little way behind him to see how he was doing. She even took it a step further one time. She asked a town police officer to stop him, even though he wasn't breaking any laws, and explain that his mother had asked the officer to check up on him. She reasoned it would teach him not to panic when he sees swirling red lights behind him. She also figured it would be a good idea for him to be just a little paranoid that his mother might have put out an APB on him and every cop was on the lookout in case he messed up!

> *The best car safety device is a rearview mirror with a cop in it.*
>
> —DUDLEY MOORE

TEEN EMBARRASSMENT

Teens have a very low embarrassment tolerance level. It is tested early and often when ours attend the Texas State Fair each year. The fair is famous for its fried food—fried peanut butter and jelly sandwiches, fried Coca Cola, even fried cheesecake. Anything still not on hoof is fried and usually topped off with a shake of powdered sugar just for flair. The sheer volume of potentially artery-clogging items available would make even the KFC colonel question the sanity of such cuisine. Texans embrace it, and I confess to having downed more fried Coke than I'd like to admit. The other fascinating displays at the fair are the livestock and the attire worn at livestock competitions by both humans and animals. It's the only place I've seen donkeys dressed in outfits to match their owners'.

> *The rate at which a person can mature is directly*
> *proportional to the embarrassment he can tolerate.*
>
> —DOUG ENGELBART

As a child I also went to the Minnesota State Fair. The Minnesota Fair is amazing because of the people's creativity. When I was a kid, United States senator Rudy Boschwitz always had a booth at the fair. Like most of our country's lawmakers, it seems Senator Boschwitz was a very wealthy man. But he was a self-made millionaire and never lost touch with the people he represented. Each year at the fair he'd be in his dairy booth, apron on, serving milk. Not just any milk, mind you. He was a milk aficionado. He could do things with milk that no one thought about back then. He had cherry-flavored milk, blueberry-flavored milk, and banana-flavored milk. This was a man who loved milk and wanted to share his passion.

If there is anything that makes people get a little crazy at a state fair, it's free food . . . or milk. They jostle for position in line, call everyone in the family to come over and cut in line, and then ask for seconds. Because of this, the state fair is also where you are guaranteed to see teens trying to be as detached from their families as possible.

"Hey, kids, let's head over to the Ag barn and learn about the reproductive cycle of the potbellied pig! The next show is in a half hour!"

> *Watching your daughter being collected by her date feels*
> *like handing over a million dollar Stradivarius to a gorilla.*
>
> —JIM BISHOP

Last year our teens practically tried to sell themselves off to another family at the Domestic Animal barn. They had a trick dog show every two hours, and the three- and four-year-olds begged to go see it. As we sat there watching FiFi twirl at her master's command, the little ones were doing their best to communicate with the dogs in dog language, by barking. At least they were trying to recreate the sound of barking. At that age, though, the "w" sound is still pretty tough for little mouths to muster. So "woof" came out more or less "oof" which, when belted out in tandem at a preschooler's pitch and decibel level, made it sound as if the seal exhibit was being held in our row. The older kids just sank lower into their seats and started giving us the desperate look. You'd recognize it. Eyes darting in our general direction, trying to lock in with an impossible-to-misunderstand message: "Please get me out of here before all my dignity is gone."

DATING DILEMMAS

The State Fair is the last place you ever, ever want to go with your family and a date in tow, which means it's the perfect place for a parent to take a daughter and her boyfriend. My theory is to get the family embarrassment (all teens are embarrassed by their families) out in the open and over with.

While a number of girls were allowed to go out on dates when they were twelve, Laurel was limited to having a boyfriend whom she could meet at the tennis court for a game, and that was it. He didn't last long enough to even remember his name. As I recall, after the tennis game he called and asked her to go to a movie and said to assure us that his parents would be there with them. I told her she was welcome to go with him to a movie and that we would sit with his parents at the movie. Next thing you know, he didn't want to go to the movie. Somehow, I have the sneaking suspicion that his parents were not part of the cast in his picture show.

We told Laurel she was too young to go to a movie with a boy unless it was a large group of kids and a parent was chaperoning. She didn't argue about it at all, and I got the feeling that she felt relieved that the pressure had been taken off her. While I know part of her wanted to go, a larger part was probably a bit uncertain, uncomfortable, and scared. This was pushing her to do something adult—go on a date—at a very early age, and I don't think she was ready for it. When we added the conditions, he backed out. Even if he hadn't, I think she would have felt more at ease knowing that we were there with her.

Kids desperately want freedom and to be more adult, but it's frightening.

Just because they're asking for a longer leash doesn't mean they're ready for it or really want you to give it to them.

Adolescence is a period of rapid changes. Between the ages of 12 and 17, for example, a parent ages as much as 20 years.

—Author Unknown

Then, Laurel turned thirteen. The rules remained the same regarding boys and movies, but we decided to allow her to go alone to movies with girlfriends if parents dropped them off right before the movie and picked them up right when it ended. She asked to go with a friend whose parents we knew and trusted. We dropped them off, and her parents were going to pick them up.

About an hour after we got home, we received a phone call from the other girl's mother. It turns out my daughter had arranged for two boys to meet them at the theater. The boys were using bad language, and her daughter didn't feel comfortable, so she went outside and called her mom to pick her up. Her mother informed us that she had offered to take Laurel home, too, but Laurel said she was going to stay and would get a ride home with another friend—one of the boys' parents, I'm sure. The mother said she felt uncomfortable calling us but thought it was important that we know. Thank goodness for that mother!

We immediately got in the car and drove to the theater where I banged on the front doors until the frightened ticket taker opened them—I think out of concern that I would break them down if he didn't. I walked into the movie and climbed up on the stage—yes, the one in front of the screen—and called my daughter's name.

Bill Cosby once said, "Always end the name of your child with a vowel so that when you yell, the name will carry." Even without the vowel, though, the call carried. On the left-hand side of the theater I saw a head of blond hair quickly duck behind a seat and two boys race into the aisle and out of the theater. I walked down the aisle, saying hello to some of her other friends whom I saw there, took her by the arm, and escorted her out.

The boys were in the lobby, racing around like chickens with their heads cut off. They weren't quite sure what was happening, and I think they were too surprised to figure out how to react. I demanded their names and told them I'd heard they had been using bad language, which had made the other girl feel uncomfortable enough that she had to leave the show.

Next, I took my daughter out to the car. She was anxious to leave as quickly as possible before her friends saw more than they already had. She started giving me a bogus line about her friend feeling ill and leaving and that there was another girl with whom she was going to ride home. And what about the boys? Oh, they just happened to come by. She said she had no idea they would be there. Right. We grounded her from doing anything at all other than going to school for three months.

It was a year later before we had to broach the topic of boys again. Life is full of irony. Remember that boy with the dirty mouth from the movie theater? Well, two days after our meeting in the movie theater lobby, he called to apologize for his behavior in front of my daughter and her friend. It was a class move and redeemed him in my eyes. A year later, Laurel asked if George could come over. I figured he had a good idea of what he might be facing. We'd had a year to prepare for how to handle dating now and had our game plan ready. We explained to Laurel that we would allow her to see a boy, but it had to be on our conditions and at our pace.

First, he had to come over and hang out with the family. George showed up prepared. It was the fall, and Laurel told him that we are a football-loving family. It really is kind of pathetic. The boys and Joe start the day with *ESPN SportsCenter*. Weekends are planned around the games. I think God may have even scheduled our church service at 10:00 A.M. on Sunday because the boys prayed so hard to get home in time to see the noon game! We watch football all weekend. College games, pro games, reruns of the previous year's draft—you name it, we watch it. In between quarters and during commercial breaks, the boys race out the back door and recreate the plays they've just watched, then run back in.

Our son Matt can name the starting line-up of every team in the NFL. He can tell you where they went to college, what their NFL statistics are, and, if they were stand-outs in college, what their stats were then too. He knows the line on every game. While I'm not a fan of extreme amounts of TV viewing, and the kids aren't allowed to watch TV during the week, during football season I let them watch on the weekends, and if the kids keep their grades high, they get to stay up late to watch the first half of *Monday Night Football.* I rationalize it by thinking that all the stats and play configurations will somehow help their analytical and mathematical skills. I know it's lame, but that's my story, and I'm sticking to it.

Back to the boyfriend. George came over and spent the day with the family. The next weekend he did the same. The third weekend we took a short break for a basketball game. It's just as competitive as football. At the end of the game he had a black eye from trying to block a shot and finding my husband's elbow instead. He didn't cry. We did have an interesting conversation when his father, the ex-marine, came to pick him up though! We spent some time talking to his dad, who was an involved and caring parent and, a week later, met his mom, who worked outside the house full-time as well as being a full-time mom. She was equally solid. At that point, we agreed to let Laurel and George go to the movies together.

Wait, not so fast. They had to take four of Laurel's brothers with them. George handled it like a champ. No complaints. The boys really liked him. George was big and tall and always the coveted first pick when they were dividing into teams. In fact, by this point, the boys would have invited George over even if Laurel hadn't!

So how was Laurel handling it? Right after the second movie-with-the-brothers date, I told her that it would be okay to go out with him alone. I told her that, despite our first encounter, we'd gotten to really know George and that he seemed like a good kid. She replied that she really liked how we had handled everything. It wasn't what I expected to hear. Other moms who knew about our process told us it was cruel, overly protective, and mean. So why did Laurel like it? It seems weird until you understand the mind of a teenager. She explained that because George got to see her family, "warts and all," right from the start, she didn't feel embarrassed about us. It was like getting a shot from the pediatrician. All children dread the pain, but they get the shot, it's quick and, while not totally painless, the bad part is over pretty quickly, and they are healthier because of it. Laurel said that because the "dating" part of being boyfriend and girlfriend had moved so slowly, they had really developed a solid friendship. She felt comfortable with him, and he felt comfortable around the family.

The movie *So I Married an Axe Murderer* runs through your mind when your daughter or son starts to date. It's a new experience. While you can't force teens to like someone you've picked out (I tried) you can give them some advice. *Tip: try to make it appear as if it's not advice!* Ask them about the person's reputation. Find out how the person treats other people. Has the person dated a lot of other people in the past? Is it a person who has demonstrated support for your teen, such as being a study buddy or cheering her on at a game? Does the person make your teen feel better about herself? Red flags are if the person is abusive, physically or verbally, to anyone. Jealousy or the desire to be with your teen all the time can mistakenly be viewed positively by your teen but often leads to unhealthy relationships. Beware of anyone who tries to negatively impact the contact between your teen and the rest of the family. Hopefully, you can use your own marriage to show your teen that a good relationship is built on mutual respect and support.

WHAT ABOUT CURFEWS?

When it comes to curfews, parents and children live in different time zones! No matter what curfew you set, your child will argue it's too early, usually by a couple of hours. The basic underlying question is whether curfews work. Do they keep young people from getting into trouble?

> *Teenagers complain there's nothing to do,*
> *then stay out all night doing it.*
>
> —BOB PHILLIPS

A 1997 report from the U.S. Conference of Mayors concludes that curfews for teens are effective in reducing vandalism and gang violence. Some 347 cities were surveyed, and 80 percent of those cities have curfews for teenagers, which usually begin around 11:00 P.M. Twenty-six cities compiled crime statistics that show that teen crime dropped an average of 21 percent once a curfew was implemented.

Even though you can demonstrate that a curfew will help (not guarantee) to avoid trouble, kids won't like it. Make sure they know you are not trying to ruin their fun. I know it sounds obvious, but they need to hear it from you, because it's the first thing they'll accuse you of doing. Explain that there isn't anything wrong with having to be home at a certain time. If they still feel embarrassed, I tell the kids to blame me. I instruct them to tell their friends I'm such a mean mother and so strict that it's just not worth it to break curfew. Take the onus off the kids by letting them dump the responsibility on you. Remember that it's tough being a teen.

TEENAGE CREATIVITY

From M. V. in Montana:

Our son was about sixteen or seventeen and had a midnight curfew on weekends. This was the age before cell phones. Just before midnight the phone rang. I, as usual, had not been totally asleep. Like most moms I sleep with one eye and one ear open until the kids arrive home. I answered the phone and heard my son say, "I've got it, Mom." I answered, "OK, honey. I didn't realize you were home." Then I hung up, rolled over and was out like a light. Perhaps, you've already figured it out. He wasn't home at all. He would simply call the house and say that when I picked up so that I would think he was home.

Kids always want greater trust and responsibility. Explain that when they are able to follow curfew rules, they are building the trust that will allow you to give them more freedom. The idea is that they are sacrificing now for a bigger payoff later. You are certain to hear that so-and-so's parent doesn't give him a curfew. First, I always like to check that out. Although I don't think you should let other parents' choices determine your own, by hearing what curfews other families have imposed, you can judge whether you might be a bit too strict. As your teen ages, you need to consider extending the curfew times. Or if your child brings up a family that doesn't have curfews, ask him to take a closer look at the child. Chances are the child runs wild. Permissive parents think that since they have given their teens responsibility, they will necessarily behave in a responsible manner. It just doesn't work that way.

Your teen, my teen, everyone's teen will break curfew at some point. One of the best rules in a nonpermissive household is that for each thirty minutes over curfew they're late, it equals one day of grounding. That day preferably should be a Friday or Saturday. For shorter periods of time, only five or ten minutes late, try trimming their curfews in the future. Say, being ten minutes tardy means a half hour earlier curfew the next time they go out. It may seem counterintuitive to force teens to spend more time at home at a point in their lives when your only quiet time comes when they are out of the home! Conversely, after teens meet curfew a number of times, you may want to let them add fifteen minutes or a half hour to their curfews. The key is to balance freedom with confinement until you can confidently set your children loose in the world, trusting they will make wise, rational choices.

You're laughing aren't you? No child is ever fully prepared to do that; then again, neither are most parents, but it's your job to safeguard your children, prepare them, and let them practice before pulling off the training wheels.

IT'S PARTY TIME!

When your child blows the candles on his fourteenth birthday cake, the party never really ends. At least he doesn't want it to. Parties today are not like the parties you and I went to. The advent of instant messaging and cell phones has forever changed the party scene. Most parents can tell you about a horror event that either occurred or was barely avoided in their home.

One time, just once, during high school I was allowed to throw a party. It was the end of the football season, and I wanted to invite the school over for a party. Keep in mind I attended a very small rural school. My mother said okay; my father flipped out. I didn't have to worry about kids from other high schools showing up since the next closest school was more than thirty miles away. I remember my mom going out to check the yard to see if someone was trying to sneak in liquor, which, of course, he was. You couldn't sneak *anything* past my mother. While the party was loud, it didn't get too wild, because there simply weren't enough kids for it to spin out of control.

That is not the case today. In less than five minutes a party can go from five kids to fifty or more. Probably the greatest problem when a child's parents are divorced is that the rules can vary widely, depending on which house it is. Laurel's father is more open about parties, and due to text messaging, kids just keep coming . . . and coming . . . and coming. There are too many kids for any parent, even with help, to supervise. The result is that the parties are loud and boisterous. A number of nonpermissive parents stopped letting their kids attend.

So Laurel, always innovative, switched tactics. She had kids with nonpermissive parents tell them that the party was at my house. It was a pretty good scheme. Their parents would be none the wiser because those kids would then get a ride to her dad's house with kids whose parents didn't mind the scene. Only one thing tripped her up. Like-minded parents are your greatest ally. Make pacts with them. Watch their backs and have them watch yours. And always, always verify a party. One mom, and then another, called me to make sure I was aware of the party and would be there to chaperone. Several even offered to help chaperone.

"Party, what party?" was my reply. Caught! The party went on because her dad was fine with it, but I had Laurel call as many parents as possible to make sure they were aware it was not at our home.

Near the end of school last year, Laurel called from a game at about 9:00 P.M. and asked if she could invite a few people to come over to our house. I asked how many, and she said twenty-five. I told her fifteen was the maximum, and she said fine. By the time twenty showed up, it became clear the party plans had spread. People who were invited had called people who weren't invited, and it simply snowballed. Some of the invited guests hadn't even arrived, and she was already over limit. I told her I was closing off the driveway and putting up a sign saying the party was closed. She was mortified.

"Everyone will hate me. They'll think I'm a loser. They've invited their friends, and this will make them look bad," she sobbed.

Tough. At this point it's really hard to be a nonpermissive parent. I knew she could head to her dad's house and invite everyone and their brother. Everyone would come, and she'd be happy. It's true that you sometimes fear losing your child because you have rules. It takes a very mature child to choose restrictions. The thorny problem for Laurel, though, was that a number of kids she really liked weren't allowed to attend parties at her dad's house because the parties got too big. If she wanted those people to show up, the party had to be at my house. It was hard to stick to my guns, but I did. I figured it would be one of those painful, but effective lessons. I explained that, if you are going to have a small party, you have to let the people you invite know that, if they invite anyone else, that person will be barred. Chances are that they won't put themselves in that position, but if they do, it's their own fault. I stationed my husband at the front door, and Laurel managed to have a normal party.

You may not be able to control what goes on elsewhere, but you *are* in charge of what happens at your house. Your teen should and will chafe at the bit because you have rules. You'll be tempted to give in, go with the flow, and "just get along," but as history and numerous studies show, a child brought up with rules in a structured environment will have fewer problems and a better relationship with his parents.

Stick to your guns! You won't have to do it too long. After all, before you know it, your teens will have survived dating, driving, and other death-defying acts. They'll be adults and out on their own. And that's where the wisdom of your nonpermissive parenting style will exhibit itself—there and in the smile on your face.

The thing that impresses me most about
America is the way parents obey their children.
—EDWARD, DUKE OF WINDSOR

The Not-So-Good, the Pretty Bad, and the Really Ugly

The self is not something ready-made, but something in continuous formation through choice of action.

—John Dewey

I was at a luncheon a few years back and began talking to a friend. Her son had gone off to a very posh, highly selective boarding school a few months earlier. It was one of those prep schools on the East Coast that everyone knows will lead to an acceptance into a good college. I asked her how he was enjoying it, and she said, "Oh, he's back home. He got kicked out." Of course, I asked why, and she explained that he'd been caught smoking pot. Then she stunned me. "Can you imagine that? Kicking a kid out for a little pot smoking? Who didn't smoke pot when they were that age?"

Maybe you're tempted to skip this chapter. Don't. You may think there are certain problems that only affect other people, other families. In fact, it's likely that it's an issue in your own home, and you don't even know it. You might say to yourself, "My daughter [or son] knows how averse I am to underage drinking and would never do it, and if she did, I would certainly know about it." You may also think the same thing about drugs. Chances are you're wrong. And I've got the statistics to prove it. Or you may be just the opposite, "Underage drinking? What's the big deal?" I'm blown away by some parents' attitude and how often I see it.

To the woman at the luncheon whose son was smoking pot, I responded that there are plenty of people who don't smoke pot at that age. But even that is beside the point. People use bad behavior, whether their own or someone else's, to excuse more bad behavior. The mom had smoked pot as a teen; therefore, it wasn't wrong that her son smoked pot.

Some people either have their heads buried in the sand or they just don't get it. Watch the news, read a paper, educate yourself. The pot you may have smoked isn't the pot your kids will smoke. Children are dying at ridiculous rates due to the stuff that is being put into drugs to make them more addictive or more profitable. Drug dealers couldn't care less what they use to cut the stuff. Yes, they'd like to keep your kid alive so they continue to get their business, but if they can hook them faster by spiking the drugs with an additive, they'll do it in a heartbeat. The parents' attitude is that since *they* smoked pot and turned out fine, what harm can it do their kids? Plenty! Since that time there have been numerous studies done that show the effect on the brain of pot smoking, or using cocaine, heroin, or LSD. The National Institute on Drug Abuse says this:

Inhalants, such as glue, gasoline, hair spray, and paint thinner, are sniffed. The effect on the brain is almost immediate. And while some vapors leave the body quickly, others will remain for a long time. The fatty tissues protecting the nerve cells in the brain are destroyed by inhalant vapors. This slows down or even stops neural transmissions. Effects of inhalants include diminished ability to learn, remember, and solve problems.[1]

> *Cocaine isn't habit-forming.*
> *I should know—I've been using it for years.*
>
> —TALLULAH BANKHEAD

Cocaine is highly "reinforcing": when it is given to animals, they will give it to themselves. In fact, if animals are given the choice, they will put up with electrical shocks and give up food and water if they can get cocaine.[2]

My friend just didn't get it. She was stunned that her son would be kicked out for "a little pot smoking." Many parents who live in that region of the country would give their eye teeth for their kids to get into top prep schools. To their credit, these schools have strict alcohol and zero-tolerance drug policies. Parents see the long lists of rules the children must abide by and assume that means their kids will follow them. To the schools' and parents' detriment, the rules are infrequently enforced. Some of the adults in charge of keeping check on dorm life are drug users themselves and are unlikely to turn in any kid. For a child to get caught and kicked out for smoking pot it means the incident must have been incredibly blatant.

I don't know. I never smoked Astroturf.

—TUG MCGRAW, WHEN ASKED IF HE
PREFERRED GRASS OR ARTIFICIAL TURF, 1974

ZERO-TOLERANCE?

My son Matt was just at a summer academic camp. No, he doesn't have bad grades, but we felt he needed some extra help getting prepared for high school math, so we sent him to what is considered one of the best summer enrichment programs available. It was held at a top-notch prep school.

Before dropping the kids off for the five-week session, parents and children had to read and sign a strongly worded zero-tolerance alcohol and drug agreement. We visited Matt one weekend and took him out to breakfast where, kind of as an aside, I asked him if there was any drug use at the school. Truly, it's sometimes amazing what your kids will say if you just take the time to ask them questions. His answered shocked me. Of the forty kids in his dorm, he said at least thirty smoked pot daily.

How? This school is in the middle of a town in the middle of nowhere. The closest grocery store is a fifteen-minute drive on a road with no traffic. You get the idea. So where could a kid go to buy drugs? He said that some parents picked up their kids when they got out of classes at 1:00 P.M. on Saturday and took them home for the night, since the kids didn't have to be back for meetings until Sunday night. While home, the kids would restock their drug stash and bring it back to the school where they'd use it themselves and sell it to others.

I doubt any of their parents were in the drug trade and were using the kids as sellers. Obviously, the parents never checked their kids' bags when they took them back to school. Why wouldn't every parent check their kids' belongings? Is it because their children would never have anything they weren't supposed to have? Guess again. Is it because the parents simply don't want to find out what might be inside? Possibly, since that would mean they would have to admit their children used drugs or alcohol, and the parents would have to deal with it. It would take time, and it might be difficult. Or they want their children to feel they are trusted. If they checked their children's backpacks, the children might get upset and feel their parents don't have unquestionable faith in them. Even kids who have done everything else right in life can slip at times. It's a parent's job—yes, j-o-b—to make sure they are there to catch children when they make mistakes. You must help them understand why it's harmful to them and work with them to change their behavior.

As I continued talking to Matt about the drugs at the dorm, I questioned why the kids weren't caught. If the majority of children are smoking pot, why does no one on the staff realize it? He said that the counselors, who were barely out of college, smoked pot, too, so they couldn't turn in a kid without the risk of being turned in themselves.

A week later the session ended, and I had the advisor-parent meeting. After talking about his progress in math and study skills, I said that I felt the administration at the school needed to know about the extent of the drug use. She said she was shocked to hear there was any drug use at all and promised to let the head of the school know about Matt's experience.

> *There must be a happy medium between*
> *being totally informed and blissfully unaware.*
>
> —DOUG LARSON

LESSONS WORTH LEARNING

Here are some lessons to be learned from this:

1. *Talk to your children about everything—sex, drugs, rock and roll.* Ask specific, pointed questions and keep asking them until you get specific, clear answers. Simply talking to your children, not once, but on a regular basis about these issues has a great impact on their behavior. If you don't say it's wrong, and they see everyone else doing it, then why shouldn't they try it too? It's not a school or a teacher's responsibility to teach your children to "Just say no." It's *your* job. You are the most important ongoing influence in their lives. What you say does matter, whether you realize it or not.

2. *Don't give your parenting responsibilities to someone else and expect them to do a good job.* If you don't care enough about your children to teach them what is right and wrong, healthy or unhealthy, why should anyone else? Don't expect that you can put them in a *safe* environment and trust it actually to be safe. If there is a will, there is a way.

3. *Remember, the so-called quality of the children around your children means nothing.* Drug use and alcoholism do not bypass rich or well-mannered kids. Some of the busiest drug-trafficking routes are from poor inner cities out to the wealthiest neighborhoods in America. Matt's roommate at summer camp was the *scholarship* kid from a low-income, all minority neighborhood. He clearly had talent and parents who cared about his education, and they

had applied for a scholarship to this summer school. Still, we are conditioned to assume that a child like that would easily be swept up in this behavior. In fact, he was in the minority of kids there who *didn't* use drugs. Do you want to see the truth about drug and alcohol use? Rent the movie *Traffic.* There are some seedy, violent, dark movies that come out of Hollywood that really can perform a public service. Every parent should watch this and realize it hits the mark. As a crime reporter and a volunteer at my local police precinct in New York City, I saw the same scenes almost daily.

4. *No child is perfect.* Teens make mistakes and they need you to realize it and help them. Check their bags, check their purses, check their drawers and closets. I started doing checks early and still do them often. Do your job and explain to them that you do these things because you realize good kids make mistakes, and you want to learn about it when they fall so you can be there to help them get back on the right track. You do it because you love them.

From my numerous discussions with my children about drug and alcohol use, the one thing that has surprised me the most is how relieved they seem to be to share what is happening. It's tough to be a kid. There are lots of temptations, and there is frequent pressure. Your children won't be approached just one time. They'll be put in positions where they can make the wrong choices numerous times, which is why one talk isn't enough. They will see kids do the wrong thing and face no consequences. You need to be a solid, dependable resource for them. Unfortunately, the most recent data suggests that parents are discussing the dangers of addictive substances less instead of more frequently with their teens. And that's definitely a step in the wrong direction.

CAN WE TALK?

The nineteenth annual *Partnership Attitude Tracking Study* shows a 12 percent decline from 2005 in the frequent discussions (four or more) between parents and their teens about the dangers of drug and alcohol abuse (55 percent in 2005 down to 49 percent in 2006). Only half of parents, 54 percent, reported thoroughly discussing the use of drugs like heroin, cocaine, and crack with their kids.[3] You may wonder whether discussions make a difference. If you've talked to them once and done a thorough job, why would you need to repeat yourself? Because it matters. You can say the same thing over and over, and your kids may complain you're doing exactly that, but the fact is that talking works.

> *Discussion is an exchange of knowledge;*
> *argument is an exchange of ignorance.*
>
> —ROBERT QUILLEN

Timetotalk.org is a wonderful resource site designed to empower parents by guiding them through the process of talking to teens about addictions. Here's what Debbie Kellogg, director of corporate relations and alliances, says:

> Research continues to show that kids who learn a lot about the risks of drugs at home are up to 50 percent less likely to use drugs, yet only 31 percent of kids report learning about the risks of drugs from their parents. Teens report that foremost among the reasons they don't use drugs is because they don't want to disappoint their parents. We want to help parents better understand that they are a huge influence on the choices kids make for themselves.[4]

HINDSIGHT IS 20/20

There are some things you simply don't realize as a kid and are surprised to find out later. When I was in high school, I had a girlfriend whose mom let her do anything she wanted. She didn't have a curfew, she didn't have to go to church, and there were no house rules. I don't know if that mom realizes to this day how lucky she was. My friend was a really great kid. She could have gone off the deep end and didn't simply because she was smart enough and had a confidence that you rarely see in high school kids.

> *There are two freedoms—the false, where a man is free to do what he likes; the true, where he is free to do what he ought.*
>
> —CHARLES KINGSLEY

My friend's mother didn't really care about her schoolwork either, and although my friend earned very high grades, her mother never suggested she apply for college. A few years out of school, my girlfriend decided to do it on her own. She worked a full-time job and enrolled in a junior college.

Years later, my husband and I flew down to Houston to celebrate her thirty-fifth birthday. At the end of the party, after most of the people had left, we had a chance to sit and talk. She knew how well my career was going and how blessed I had been in life. She said to me that she always wished that her mother had been like mine.

She said, "Your mom really cared about you. You had rules, and she really kept track of you. My life would have been a lot easier if my mom had been like yours."

It was a statement I would never have expected in a million years. As a kid, I always envied her. I wished my mom was like hers! Her life seemed so carefree. She seemed lucky. With the benefit of hindsight, we both realized that I had fewer bumps along the way in large part due to good parenting. Your children may not appreciate what you do now, but at some point they will get it, and so will their friends.

When I tell my kids why they shouldn't use drugs or alcohol, I give them facts and always follow it up by explaining that I'm discussing it with them because I love them and want them to be the best human beings they can be. I also tell them very bluntly that kids whose parents don't do this simply care more about themselves than they do about their children. Either they want to be buddies with their children and are willing to abdicate their parenting responsibility, or they don't want to be bothered.

I was driving Laurel and one of her friends to town and was using the time to tell Laurel about something that she needed to try to do better, and as Laurel started protesting, the other girl said, "You're really lucky that your mom cares." I immediately thought of my own friend's statement. Your kids need and want you to be involved.

CHOOSING THE RIGHT FRIENDS

When you learn that your child's friend is using drugs or alcohol, it puts you in an uncomfortable situation. You have to label the child's behavior as *bad*, but that makes you feel guilty. You may be tempted to hope that your child will be a positive influence on the friend instead of vice versa. Don't fool yourself. The vastly greater chance is that your child will be pulled down, instead of being able to pull a friend up.

> *Do not stand in a place of danger trusting in miracles.*
> —ARABIAN PROVERB

The other child likely doesn't have parents who are willing to take the time to help guide their child. By your asking questions, your child is able to let you understand what he faces. Knowledge is power. The more you know, the easier it will be to help your child be his best. Don't fall into the trap of complacency. You think you've done a perfect job parenting. You've given your children statistics and talked to them about abuses until you're blue in the face, and it can be tempting to assume that's all it takes. But it can all fall to pieces if you allow them to hang out with kids who aren't like-minded.

HEROES OR HEELS?

Whitey Herzog said, "I'm not buddy-buddy with the players. If they need a buddy, let them buy a dog." Good philosophy! But permissive parents just don't get it. They think their teens want a buddy, a pal, a best friend. They love their children and trust them unconditionally. Even nonpermissive parents get the wool pulled over their eyes sometimes. But since we talk to our children about these issues so often, there is a greater chance we will be able to sense when we're being fleeced.

As I mentioned before, I always volunteer to be a team parent. That means I also host the team dinner at the end of the season. Nonpermissive parents know that teens like to party alone, but by adding their parents into the mix, you can increase the odds of having a noneventful evening, which is what you want.

I invited the entire football team—along with parents and coaches—over to our house at the end of last year's season. I gave the kids some space. They had pizza, chips, and sodas in the family room while the parents had lasagna in the dining room. We turned on ESPN for them to watch, and I pulled out some finger-flicking football games for the boys to play. The grand prize was an autographed pro football.

I went back and forth to check on the kids, but I didn't notice when two of the boys disappeared. I realized my son was irritated after the dinner and asked why. He was angry because what they did made him feel uncomfortable. I also think he was disappointed that I hadn't figured out what was going on.

It turns out the two boys had gone into the toddlers' playhouse in the backyard to smoke pot. You might assume their parents would figure this out on the way home, based on the smell and their children's behavior. Nope. In fact, one dad, who is a friend of my husband's, is convinced that his son's problem (his line was that his son had gone through some "issues") had been handled and was over. Even though the parents, especially the dad, are very involved in the school and the son's life, they are classic permissive parents. They are simply unaware and in denial about the extent of the son's problems, or they don't view it as a serious enough problem even though the boy does poorly in class and may be repeating a grade. The parents of the other boy seem to be nonpermissive parents, but I think they've let their guards down, just as I did that evening. My children say their boy was a good kid until recently. He began hanging out with the other boy, and the next thing they knew, he was smoking pot daily too.

So what do you do if you use drugs yourself? First of all, you need help yourself. Obviously, you can't tell your kids, "Do as I say, not as I do." Maybe you think that you *handle* your problem, so it's okay. *Maybe* you do, although I immediately think of that drug public service advertisement from the 1980s, which features a person saying, "When I grow up, I want to be a drug addict." No one wants to grow up to be an addict, but it just happens all too easily, especially in people who think they can control themselves and drugs. As I've shown, you are the greatest influence in your children's lives. As Roy L. Smith said, "We are apt to forget that children watch examples better than they listen to preaching." So be a hero, not a heel.

> *Reality is a crutch for people who can't cope with drugs.*
> —Lily Tomlin

FACING THE CONSEQUENCES

A friend of mine told me a story about an acquaintance who smokes pot frequently. He is very, very successful and, frankly, brilliant intellectually. One would have an impossible time arguing that his pot smoking has impacted his intellectual capacity or his ability to earn a huge salary, which has also enabled him to give millions of dollars to philanthropic organizations.

But all drug use has consequences, intended or not. His children have dabbled in drugs, and one has done a bit more. It has brought ruin to his young life. He is unable to function well in school. While he may be able to get into college, due to his parent's connections, there is no doubt that he will have a tough time. He might get a job, again thanks to his parents, but he will have a difficult time succeeding. His brain may be permanently damaged, due to the high quantities of drugs he has taken. Even this hasn't diminished his father's drug use.

Further, the habit is hurting other families. My friend complains to me that when she talks to her children about not doing drugs, they reply, "But your friend does it." The man also, apparently, keeps his pot in an easily accessible place, and the kids, including my friend's son, go with his son to the house and take it. Unintentionally, he is fueling another batch of drug users and hurting another family. In every other way this man is smart, generous, kind, and a good influence, and so she is baffled by his behavior. Drug use has unintended consequences. His own and other people's children are getting sucked in by following his poor example.

> *The best pitch I ever heard about cocaine was back*
> *in the early eighties when a street dealer followed*
> *me down the sidewalk going, "I got some great*
> *blow man. I got the stuff that killed Belushi."*
>
> —DENNIS LEARY

BAD NEWS, GOOD NEWS

During 2006 there were 977,000 new cocaine users in the United States. The average age of those who first used cocaine was 20.3 years. According to the 2006 National Survey on Drug Use and Health, approximately 35.3 million Americans aged twelve and older had tried cocaine at least once in their lifetimes, representing 14.3 percent of that population.[5]

There is some positive news, though. During 2000 there were an estimated 2,707,000 chronic cocaine users and 3,035,000 occasional cocaine users in the United States; yet, according to "What America's Users Spend on Illegal Drugs," users spent $35.3 billion on cocaine in 2000, a decrease from the $69.9 billion spent in 1990. Americans consumed 259 metric tons of cocaine in 2000, a decrease from the 447 metric tons consumed in 1990.[6]

JUST SAY NO . . . TO MOM AND DAD?

In college one of my girlfriends would come back from school breaks and tell me about smoking pot and using cocaine with her mother. She lived in an American city known for its good times, and she thought her mom was really cool. Oddly enough, my friend never did any kind of drugs at school and, other than telling her roommate, I don't think she shared what went on during breaks with anyone else. She realized that it went against the social norms at Southern Methodist University (SMU) at that time. If she had done drugs, she would have been ostracized. This made it even stranger that her mother would do drugs with her at home. When she would tell me about this, the thought that always ran through my mind was, *Wow, I feel sorry for her.* The pressure from peers nowadays is tough enough for kids to resist. Imagine needing to say no to your mom.

I assume that a very small percentage of parents actually try to get their children to use drugs or alcohol, but are they doing enough to prevent it? According to the Partnership for a Drug-Free America, 98 percent of parents say they've talked to their children about drugs, yet only 27 percent of teens say they've learned a lot from their parents about the risk of using drugs. According to The Century Council, when it comes to underage drinking, literally millions of parents are in the dark:

- 16 percent of 13- to 15-year-old girls say they drink with friends, but only 5 percent of mothers think their daughters are drinking.

- 30 percent of 16- to 18-year-old girls say they drink with their friends, but only 9 percent of their mothers think they are drinking.
- 51 percent of 19- to 21-year-old girls say they drink with friends, but only 32 percent of their mothers think they are drinking.[7]

What this proves is that millions of parents in America are absolutely clueless about whether their children are underage drinkers or not. Although these are statistics from only one state, they are indicative of the issue in every state in the Union.

A case in point is what happened at one teenager's Sweet 16 party in Massachusetts. *Sweet?* I'm not so sure about that. *Wild* would be a better choice of words. While the parents sat upstairs with friends at their country club, the children brought in kegs of beer. Just an hour into the party, the police were called while the parents sat blissfully unaware of anything going on around them. Kids were wasted. Kids became violent. One boy who was graduating that spring threw a punch at a police officer. His acceptance into one of the most prestigious universities in the country was revoked the moment charges of assaulting a police officer were filed. His father's money, connections, and pleading couldn't get his son back in. In their eyes, at least, their son not going to Harvard meant his life had been ruined. The parents who threw the party were well-intentioned people, who either didn't think underage drinking would happen at their daughter's party or were unable to control the party they threw, so they ignored the obvious.[8]

> *Complete abstinence is easier than perfect moderation.*
>
> —ST. AUGUSTINE

In Westchester County, New York, which is just outside New York City, teen drinking is far too common, and according to numerous news reports, it is drinking done with the parents' permission. On New Year's Eve in 2002, twenty-six teens—ages fifteen to nineteen—were arrested at a hotel for possession of alcohol and marijuana. The father of one of the kids had rented the room but told police his son had promised there wouldn't be any alcohol. Making his alleged naiveté even more shocking is the fact that his older son had previously been found dead in a river following a night of drinking.[9]

In Illinois, two eighteen-year-olds were killed in a car crash after drinking at a party after the high school's homecoming game. The parents routinely let their son throw parties. Not surprisingly, he also had two prior convictions for underage drinking, but the parents let him continue throwing parties until two friends died, and the prosecutor filed charges against the parents. During the court case, prosecutors proved that the parents had, in fact, tried to hide the evidence, which was beer cans, and shield their son's role in the party. They were convicted of endangerment of a child and obstruction of justice for lying to police. They faced a maximum of one year in jail. They let the kids drink in their house. Two kids were dead. Yet they reportedly showed absolutely no emotion when the verdict was read.[10]

In Somers, New York, a couple and their adult son were charged with letting kids drink at their home during a high school graduation party. Police were tipped off to the party after one of the underage girls, who had been drinking at the party, passed out on a neighbor's porch, and he called an ambulance.

In Montgomery County, Maryland, police reported that when they responded to a teenage drinking party, they witnessed one of the kids' mothers run to warn the other children that the police were coming. Both parents were given civil citations.

In June 2007, a fifteen-year-old girl in Tarrytown, New York, told police she was gang-raped by male friends she had been drinking with at a party.

The first thing in the human personality
that dissolves in alcohol is dignity.
—AUTHOR UNKNOWN

WITH MY PARENTS' PERMISSION

Any reading above 0.00 on an alcohol screening test is generally sufficient to convict a teenager in most states. The reaction? Parents still don't get it! Police are frustrated because some parents tell police they didn't view under-age drinking as a problem while others seem to think the problem is inflated. Here are more statistics from The Century Council:

- 49 percent of mothers of teenage girls say it is okay for their daughters to drink
- 38 percent of mothers say it is okay for their daughters to drink on special occasions
- 20 percent of mothers say drinking alcohol is a natural part of growing up[11]

> *Vice is a creature of such hideous mien . . .*
> *that the more you see it the better you like it.*
>
> —FINLEY PETER DUNNE

Some parents are fully knowledgeable about what happens and say they would rather have their kids drinking in their own home than not know where they are. An example is what happened in May 2002, just outside Providence, Rhode Island, where teen drinking was common.

At West Warwick High School during the 2001–2002 school years, students indicated in a survey that 44 percent of them had been drinking in the past month. According to an interview in azcentral.com, Gregg Anderson says his parents routinely let him have a couple of friends over for evenings of drinking and card playing. When he and his friends planned an all-night beer keg bash at a beach forty minutes from his home, his parents, William and Patricia Anderson, worried that the kids would drive drunk. They decided to offer to host the party at their house instead.

William collected the kids' car keys when they arrived. Throughout the evening, until 4:30 A.M., when police closed it down, the kids did "keg stands"—that's where they drink beer directly and quickly from the keg taps—while others guzzled yard glasses, which hold twenty-four ounces. Mr. Anderson was arrested for providing alcohol to minors, but the charges were later dropped.[12]

While the parents certainly prevented drunk-driving deaths that night, one of the long-term messages they sent to all of the children is that it's okay to break the law and help others do so, and it's okay to drink potentially lethal levels of alcohol.

FROM HOUSE TO HOUSE

The bottom line is that you have to think long and hard about any choice you make regarding your children and alcohol. My sister, Adrienne, has a friend who is divorced with a son. The son shares the homes of both parents on a weekly basis. The man, from time to time, allows his son to drink a beer with him while he is home and under his direct supervision. But one time the man's son brought his girlfriend over to the house while his dad was gone. They basically enjoyed the fruits of the liquor cabinet and the hot tub.

> *If you know someone who tries to drown their sorrows,*
> *you might tell them sorrows know how to swim.*
>
> —H. JACKSON BROWN JR.

When the girl returned tipsy to her parents' home, her father was obviously upset. The girl's father contacted an attorney, which resulted in charges against the boy's father for contributing to the delinquency of a minor. The thought process behind the charge was that the boy's father had allowed them access to the liquor cabinet without supervision; therefore, he was responsible.

The boy's father then got an attorney to defend himself. The attorney wondered how the son gained access to the house. It was explained that the son had a key to the house, but there was a rule that he was only allowed into the house when his father was there. The son had never broken the rule (as far as his dad knew) until this incident.

The man's attorney advised that because the son did not have permission to be in the home while his father was away, the dad should file breaking-and-entering charges against his own son. If he were to file charges against his own son, the same charges could then be filed against his son's girlfriend since she was also then in the home without permission. Although a very difficult thing to do, the father filed charges against his own son and his son's girlfriend. The charges would most certainly result in a conviction against the girl as she, her father, and the son had already admitted she had been in the man's home. Realizing the jeopardy, the girlfriend's father dropped the charges against the boyfriend's father, which resulted in the charges being dropped against his daughter. The two parents proceeded to amicably work out their differences between themselves and their children.

> *First you take a drink, then the drink takes*
> *a drink, then the drink takes you.*
> —FRANCIS SCOTT FITZGERALD

I read an online student high school newspaper featuring a discussion about teen drinking. A student, who declared himself a "connoisseur of beer," said he began drinking early in life because his parents wanted him to appreciate alcohol and not view it as something to binge on. The student wrote that his parents don't mind him drinking as long as he doesn't get slobbering drunk.

So they're fine with their son getting drunk, just not "slobbering" drunk.

I have the suspicion that this isn't the message his parents thought they were sending, but parental acceptance of illegal behavior is a slippery slope. In fact, parents who "understand kids are just being kids" may be the problem. According to the *Journal of Studies on Alcohol*, parents' attitudes of acceptance about drinking have been associated with adolescents' initiating and continuing drinking. The North Carolina Department of Crime Control and Public Safety conducted a large study, which showed that nearly half of all mothers in that state said it was okay for their daughters to drink. In North Carolina 75 percent of all high school students say they drink, and 33 percent say they started before they were eleven years old.[13] According to the National Institute on Alcohol Abuse and Alcoholism, children who start drinking with friends before age fifteen are four times more likely to become alcoholic adults.[14]

If you read any online student blogs, your eyes will be opened to the prevalent attitude teens have toward underage drinking. I read a story from a boy who claims his dad bought a Breathalyzer so he could test kids who left his house after a party. While he didn't provide alcohol to the kids, he also didn't mind drinking parties at his house. The dad's theory was that he'd rather have them drinking at his house than somewhere else. When kids got drunk he'd let them stay overnight or drive them home himself. The son commends his dad for providing a safe place for kids to get drunk.

What I surmise is that the kid and his friends drink irresponsibly, which negates the permissive-parenting argument that drinking at home helps children control their drinking.

There are a couple of reasons why his dad's choice is wrong. The first, and perhaps most important, is that his dad is telling him he can pick and choose which laws to uphold and which laws are acceptable to break. In fact, his dad's own criminal behavior of knowingly allowing underage drinking, sometimes to the extreme, is held up as an example of good parenting. Why would any kid think he needs to abide by the law if his parents are more than willing to break it?

LEGALLY SPEAKING

I understand the theory behind the parent's reasoning, but I think the extent to which he carried it is dangerous. I grew up in a small, very conservative town where the Baptist church basically held a monopoly. It was and still is a lovely place where common sense prevails, and parents are involved in their children's lives to a great extent. But here was my experience. At that time the legal age limit for drinking was eighteen, which meant many high school seniors were legal to drink. Therefore, it was not uncommon to see alcohol at a party, since some of the kids were old enough to drink. Many of their parents didn't approve of alcohol at all . . . for anyone. For some, dancing was not far behind on the list of sinful behaviors. The children who came from families that forbid alcohol were often the kids who were sneaking out to get, as Nicholas says, "slobbering drunk" both before and after they were eighteen.

> *The chief reason for drinking is the desire to behave in a certain way, and to be able to blame it on alcohol.*
>
> —MIGNON MCLAUGHLIN

My parents thought long and hard about how to handle the issue of alcohol with us. Two factors influenced their decision. First, one of my parents' fathers was an alcoholic and, second, we traveled internationally a great deal, especially in Germany and Italy where, at the time, it was not uncommon for kids to have a small glass of wine or even beer at an evening meal. They felt that the mystique of alcohol was the biggest lure for underage kids. So when we were about twelve, they started letting us have a sip of wine if it was being served at dinner. At about fifteen, we were allowed to have about one-eighth cup of wine in our own glasses, if they were having it at dinner. The alcohol was consumed at home with family at a meal, not at a party. No one was allowed to drive afterward. No alcohol was served if our friends were over. I had gotten my hardship driver's license at a very early age, and barring drinking and driving was a key provision and lesson.

I want to emphasize that there is a huge difference between having a sip of wine at home with your parents and partying on down with your pals. A study released in 2008 by John E. Donovan, an associate professor of psychiatry and epidemiology at the University of Pittsburgh, shows that by age ten, of the children studied, roughly half had sipped or tasted alcohol. There did not seem to be any link to delinquent or other problem behavior later on. On the flip side, studies seem to reveal that kids who drink—not sip or taste—alcohol have "higher levels of disinhibition, more positive alcohol expectancies, more peer alcohol use, and lower school grades."[15]

From M. C. in Texas:

I have two boys old enough to drive. When it comes to drinking, my policy is that if the kids ever get behind the wheel after drinking, they will never drive one of my cars again . . . ever. The door has always been kept open, allowing the kids to call whenever they need to be picked up from someplace and brought home, with no questions asked. While I would prefer they don't drink, I know that kids make mistakes. I don't want their mistakes to be deadly ones for themselves or someone else. The lesson is hopefully learned to be in more control the next time and not drink.

While everyone knows the legal drinking age is twenty-one in the United States, there are various exceptions in many states which make it legal to drink at home with a parent and for religious purposes. I think my parents handled this in the best way for our family. But the concept can be abused. Here is the most common one I hear. People say they allow their kids to drink in moderation at a party and then drive, "but only if there is no one else in the car," as if that makes the choice more responsible. You might assume that since an adult who drinks in moderation is able to handle driving a car, the same would hold true for a teenager. Wrong. The crash risk for young drivers is substantially higher than for adults, especially at low and moderate blood alcohol concentrations, according to the Insurance Institute for Highway Safety (IIHS). The most stunning statistic is that the fatality rate for kids who have had one drink and then drive reaches its highest peak in the two years right before they reach legal drinking age. Most people assume the closer they are to the legal age to drink responsibly and then drive, the safer they would be.[16]

So what do you say to a parent who says underage drinking is a harmless "rite of passage"? Try sharing this statistic. According to the Hazelden Foundation, if you add underage drinking to your children's life experiences, you are also likely adding: fatal car crashes, rape, unwanted pregnancy, suicide, homicide, academic failure, vandalism, alcohol poisoning, alcoholism, and more. Drinking is associated with the leading causes of death among young people. A sixteen-year-old is more likely to die from a drinking-related problem than any other cause.[17] Death is not a rite of passage. I think, ironically enough, Dean Martin had it right when he said, "If you drink, don't drive. Don't even putt."

Even if many parents won't deal with underage drinking, towns are taking action after numerous deaths stemming from underage drunk-driving wrecks. New Jersey was the first state to adopt a "social host liability" law. Now parents in states that include Delaware, Oregon, Vermont, New Hampshire, Texas, Pennsylvania, North Dakota, New Mexico, Kansas, Minnesota, Indiana, Idaho, North Carolina, and possibly soon Illinois can be criminally prosecuted in addition to being charged for medical bills and property damages and can be sued for emotional pain and suffering.[18]

In July 2007 charges were filed against two Tampa, Florida, parents after a teenager was killed in a car wreck after drinking at their open house party.[19]

In Charlottesville, Virginia, a mother and stepfather received twenty-seven-month jail sentences for hosting a teen drinking party. Police say the parents were fully aware of what was going on.[20] In Harrison, New York, a teenager died after a night of drinking at a home party.[21]

The Center for the Study of Law Enforcement Policy in California researched underage drinking parties and found parties are getting larger and involve hundreds of kids, frequently due to the speed with which party information can get to kids via text messaging. The kids can get out the invitations, but they need the parents to get the booze. And they do.[22]

Here are some statistics that shocked me. According to a study by the Century Council, 65 percent of underage children who drink obtain the alcohol from their families and friends. In 2004, among fifteen- to twenty-year old drivers, 29 percent who were killed had been drinking.[23]

According to the 2005 National Survey on Drug Use and Health, more than one in four American kids reported they were currently drinking alcohol. One in five children says he is a binge drinker.[24]

Who is drinking?

Age 12: 3 percent	Age 15: 20 percent	Age 18: 44 percent
Age 13: 6 percent	Age 16: 27 percent	Age 19: 52 percent
Age 14: 11 percent	Age 17: 33 percent	Age 20: 58 percent[25]

The *Journal of Studies on Alcohol* shows the children are less likely to drink when their parents spend time with them and interact in a positive way with them and when their parents report feeling close to one another. Adolescents drink less and have fewer alcohol-related problems when their parents discipline them consistently and set clear expectations.[26]

WHO CARES?

Although we have had numerous discussions with our children about underage drinking, we recently found out that one of them made a very poor decision. A few friends were invited over to watch T.V., and within a short amount of time, our child began throwing up. Why? We wondered but soon found a couple of empty beer cans in the TV room. We probably wouldn't have found out until we had conducted one of our unannounced visits to the room. Unfortunately for our child, the throwing up gave it away. The other children's parents were called to let them know what happened. Then we decided how to handle it. An upcoming vacation at a resort with a kid's club had promised to be a real treat since everyone enjoys hanging out and meeting new people. So we grounded our child from going. Later—not then—the child remarked that the punishment showed we really cared.

> *Grown-ups never understand anything for themselves, and it is tiresome for children to be always and forever explaining things to them.*
>
> —ANTOINE DE SAINT-EXUPERY

Children want structure. They want rules, and they want to know someone cares enough about them to punish them. Know it. Believe it. After this experience I decided we needed a bigger game plan. Our child needed to know the punishment for making a mistake like this again would be significant, and I had to make sure it was something I had full control over enforcing. What is the one thing teens want more than anything else? Their driver's licenses. So we made the rule that if any child was caught drinking underage, we would tack on an extra six months before letting him get his license. If he did it again, it would be another six months. The thought of everyone else tooling around town in a car while being stuck calling your mom for a ride is a powerful motivator to make the right decision. Sometimes all the intellectual reasoning in the world may be forgotten in the frenzy to fit in. Knowing they will be the only ones without a driver's license, and therefore "out," is just the pinch they need to stay on the right path. So far, so good. For more information, see chapter 7, and for a driving contract, see appendix B.

From K. T. in South Carolina:

Our daughter cared nothing about school from the moment she entered ninth grade. I can't remember all the parent/teacher conferences, pleading sessions, tutors, and bouts of crying that we went through. She limped along and made it through her junior year (on the second try) and then gave up altogether. She thought she knew everything. I decided that, if she was smart enough to quit school, then she was smart enough to be on her own. She moved in with a friend and, later, a boyfriend while working as a waitress. When the boyfriend couldn't pay the rent, she called me for help. I asked if she'd gotten her GED or diploma, and she said she hadn't. She begged me to help her, and I offered only one option, to help her enroll in Job Corps. She despised the idea but realized it was her only option. She enrolled. Dropping her off was the hardest thing I'd ever done. She came home for holidays and long weekends. She graduated with a diploma and a certificate in business administration. She now works as an administrative assistant at a successful architectural firm. I know she hated me for making her go through this, but she is now grateful for having been given the chance to make things right for herself. She is twenty years old and a shining example of persistence paying off.

As I've said, I am a firm believer that the most difficult trials can result in the greatest lessons. While I believe nonpermissive parents do what they can to steer their children away from falling into the biggest holes, that's not enough. It's also not the end of the world when children do err although I know it may feel like it.

Let love overcome the anger and the disappointment. Explain to your children why their actions must change for their own personal good. Help them understand the repercussions, both intended and unintended. Make sure there is a punishment. Our goal can't be to keep our children from making any kind of mistake, because we will certainly fail. The goal must be to take their inevitable mistakes and make certain our children learn from them. After all, life is not about *being* a perfect person; it's about consistently *becoming* a better person. And with our help, as nonpermissive parents, our children can surely pursue that goal and win.

Character cannot be developed in ease and quiet. Only through experience of trial and suffering can the soul be strengthened, ambition inspired, and success achieved.

—HELEN KELLER

Conclusion

Parents who are always giving their children nothing
but the best usually wind up with nothing but the worst.

—Author Unknown

By choosing to have children, you have certainly added to your life's responsibilities. Ready or not, they need you! Parenting is a privilege. It comes with rights, but they are quickly eroding in some states. That makes your job of parenting even more difficult and even more critical.

Parenting is a blessing, and by now you know it doesn't come with a step-by-step handbook. After decades of experts telling us to raise children in the opposite way than our ancestors, because it's "better for the child," we are struggling with problems they never expected. The theories of kids having greater autonomy from parents; wearing clothing that expresses their individuality; attending open, nonjudgmental schools; and receiving unconditional approval have been an abysmal failure. The result is increasingly violent juvenile crime, extreme disobedience, staggering rates of depression, millions of children on medicine to help them behave normally, and skyrocketing obesity. Each of our children is different. If you have your children's best interests at heart, you can take the experts' advice and see if it makes sense for your kids. You innately know what your children need. Unfortunately, too many parents are willing to forego their parental job and its responsibilities. They want to focus on themselves and just "keep the peace" with their children even if that leads the children on the path to ruin.

The goal for you as a parent should be to do whatever is necessary, even when it's unpleasant and inconvenient, to raise children who will be assets to society. Give them the opportunity to fail and the encouragement to try again. The path to self-respect and self-confidence is never ending—a lifetime pursuit. And while we parents can and should do our best to help our children along the journey, ultimately it's up to them to achieve it.

Children are gifts from God. And parenting can be the most rewarding and fulfilling aspect of our lives. Best of all, because of our great love for our children, this all-important job is not a chore but a joy that lasts a lifetime.

In the long run, we shape our lives, and we shape ourselves. The process never ends until we die. And the choices we make are ultimately our responsibility.

—ELEANOR ROOSEVELT

Appendix A

Sample of Home Rules Contract

Chapter 6 refers to a contract between parent(s) and children, spelling out expected behaviors and resulting consequences. Here is a sample of that contract:

Home Rules Contract for the _____ Family

All family members who sign this contract agree to abide by the rules stated.

1. CURFEW

- You are expected to return home directly from school unless you have made prior arrangements with us.

- If you are permitted to go out on a school night, curfew time is _____.

- If you are permitted to go out on a weekend night, curfew time is _____.

Consequence if curfew is broken:

_____

2. ALCOHOL AND DRUGS:

You are not allowed to use, try, or hold for someone else any drugs, alcohol, or tobacco products.

Consequence of breaking the alcohol and drug rule:

_____

3. TELEPHONE, LAPTOP, AND COMPUTERS:

- You will not visit any Web sites with adult content.

- Cell phones will be turned off at _____ P.M.

- You will not post your phone number, address, full name, or school on any Web site.

- You will not post inappropriate photos of yourself or anyone else on any Web site.

- You will not use derogatory or bullying language on any Web site.

- You will provide a list of the social networking sites on which you have a listing.

Consequence if any of these rules are broken:

_____

4. CAR USE:

- You must make arrangements to use the car.

- You must fill up the car after using it.

- You are responsible for paying for any damages to the car.

- You are not allowed to drive the car above the speed limit or in a reckless manner.

Consequence if car use rules are broken:

_____

NOTE: For a thorough driving contract, consult Appendix B.

5. CHORES:

- You will perform these specific chores (list them below):

_____

_____

_____

_____

- As compensation you will be given _____ as an allowance.

Consequence if chores are not performed:

_____

PARENT(S):   **CHILD/CHILDREN:**

_____   _____

_____   _____

Date: _____   Date: _____

NOTE: This is a basic contract draft to which you can add or subtract, depending on the issues and changing needs in your home.

Source: Prepared by the author

Appendix B

Sample of Driving Contract

Chapter 7 refers to a driving contract for new teen drivers. It is included here, with the permission of Dale Wisely. For a downloadable version of this contract, please go to www.parentingteendrivers.com.

DRIVING CONTRACT

The new driver must initial each point to show it has been read and understood.

_____ Permission to drive is not a legal right. Getting a license from the state is not the same as having permission to drive, which is granted to me by my parents, who are under no obligation to do so, and who may withdraw the privilege at any time. I understand that I will only be allowed to drive when I abide by the rules and regulations established by my parents.

_____ **I know that driving a car is an extremely serious matter.**

_____ Automobile accidents are the leading cause of death of people 16 to 20 years old.

_____ I am more likely to die in an auto accident than from any other cause.

_____ Recklessness or errors that I make while driving could kill or hurt me, kill or hurt people in the car I drive, and kill or hurt people in other cars. I can make mistakes that will kill or hurt pedestrians and people on bicycles. Among those that could be victims of my driving mistakes are these: babies, children, my friends, my family members, and many others.

_____ I will abide by laws regulating driving. I will observe and abide by posted speed limits. I will abide by rules established by my parents. I recognize these are for my protection and the protection of others.

_____ I understand that the car I drive is the property of my parents. Even a car that is a "gift" to me is still, legally, the property of my parents. Even if I pay for it, or part of it, it belongs, legally, to my parents. I drive the car only with their permission.

_____ I understand that the terms of this driving agreement may be changed based on how I handle the freedom and responsibility of driving. The rules will get stricter if my parents feel that I am not doing well. It will get somewhat less strict if my parents agree that I am doing well.

_____ I must study and be aware of the terms of this contract. "Forgetting" any part of the contract is not an excuse.

THREE CRITICAL RULES

_____ If my parents deny me permission to drive, for whatever reason, I will abide by this and give them the keys immediately with no argument. I may ask to meet with my parent(s) no earlier than 24 hours later to talk about it. Refusal to immediately surrender the keys will result in the car being immobilized. This will be done with a steering wheel lock or some other method. *No Exceptions.* If my parents immobilize the car I drive because I did not obey the above rule, two to four weeks will pass, at my parents' choice, before any discussion will occur about driving again. Another incident of failure to surrender keys on demand will lead to indefinite suspension of driving privileges.

_____ If I drive in defiance of my parents' order not to drive, this contract is cancelled and no driving will be permitted for at least one year.

_____ If I drive in defiance of my parents' order not to drive, my parents may call the police.

Category A

These rules, if violated, will lead to indefinite suspension of driving privileges. This is the most serious set of rules. I understand that I may lose my driving privileges indefinitely if any one of these is violated even once.

1. *Alcohol/drug use not allowed.* Even though some teenagers drink, as a minor, it is illegal for me to drink alcohol. I understand that my parents do not permit me to drink. However, if I do drink, I will not drive for 24 hours after my last use of alcohol in *any* amount.

    No drug use/abuse. I will not drive for 72 hours after my last use of any "substance." In this agreement, *substance* means any drug or chemical, including but not limited to marijuana, pills, inhalants, and other drugs, which would be expected by my parents to alter my ability to drive. There is no acceptable amount of any substance of this kind. If I use any drugs, I will not drive for 72 hours. This rule may include medications prescribed to me or over-the-counter medications. In the cases of legal medications, I will inform my parents of any such medications I have taken so that they can judge whether taking these medications will interfere with my driving ability.

    Furthermore:

a. *No riding with others who have used alcohol or drugs.* I will not ride as a passenger with any driver who has used alcohol or any substance as defined above. I will not ride with anyone who it would be reasonable to think may have used alcohol or drugs.

b. *Alternatives to riding with others who have used alcohol or drugs.* If I find myself in a situation as described above, I will contact my parents or another designated adult to arrange for transportation. I understand that my parents will appreciate that behavior and will make every effort to avoid asking me a lot of questions about it.

c. *No alcohol or drugs in car.* I will not allow alcohol or illegal drugs in the car. This includes over-the-counter medications (cough medicines, for example) when I have reason to believe someone has them in their possession for purposes of abuse. My parents will hold me responsible for any alcohol or drugs in the car even if they don't belong to me or it is the fault of someone riding in my car.

2. *No thrill-seeking/stunts.* I will not engage in any thrill-seeking behavior while driving. I will not drive for recreation. Driving too fast, all kinds of racing, and any kind of "stunt" involving a car is *Not Allowed.* Driving is for transportation *only.*

3. *Informing parents about accidents and police encounters.* I will inform my parents about any and all tickets, accidents, and encounters with police (including warnings).

4. *No firearms or other weapons.* I will not drive with any guns or other deadly weapons in the vehicle. I will not ride in a car that contains firearms or other weapons. I will not ride with any person carrying guns or other weapons.

Category B

Violations will lead to suspension of driving privileges for up to three months.

1. *Permission to drive.* I must ask permission to drive each time I drive. Exceptions to this rule will be given for regularly scheduled transportation to school, work, regular meetings, and so on. I will ask permission to drive to specific locations and will discuss the route planned. I will be certain that my parents know where I am. I will not make unscheduled stops or side trips without first checking with my parents.

2. *Curfew.* I may not drive after 10:00 P.M. This curfew will be reviewed and possibly revised when I meet with my parents on _____ (scheduled date to review/revise contract).

3. *Limit on passengers.* During the first month of driving, I will not be allowed to have any passengers. I may ask permission for specific exceptions. This will be adjusted, if things go well, when we revise the contract. I will, however, continue to have limits on passengers.

4. *Off-Limits Areas.* I will not drive on streets, highways, or in areas that are designated as off-limits. I understand that greater flexibility will come as I gain experience and show that I am honoring the agreement. For the time being, the following roads and areas are to be avoided (list below):

_____

_____

_____

5. *No one else drives vehicle.* I will not permit any other person to drive the car without my parents' specific permission for each specific case.

Category C

Violations may lead to suspension of driving privileges for up to six weeks.

1. *Weather/road conditions.* I will respect weather and road conditions, slowing down as needed for safety. I will contact my parents to discuss weather or poor road conditions when I am out driving.

2. *Emotional upset.* Knowing that judgment and driving skills are altered by emotions, I will not drive when I am upset or angry. If upset, I will contact my parents for transportation, and I reserve the right to maintain my privacy regarding personal matters. My parents agree not to ask a lot of unnecessary questions.

3. *Taking care of vehicle.* It is my responsibility to protect the car I drive. I will keep it reasonably clean and maintained. I have some specific responsibilities regarding the maintenance of the car as noted below:
    a. *Passenger behavior.* I will not allow my passengers to behave in such a way as to damage the car or distract me while driving.
    b. *Seatbelts.* I will wear my seatbelt at all times and require all passengers to wear them.
    c. *Friends ride only with their parents' permission.* When transporting my friends, I will be reasonably sure that they have their parents' permission to ride with me.

d. *Thank you for not smoking.* I will not allow smoking in the car. I will not smoke in the car.

e. *No eating and driving.*

4. *Car audio system.* For the first two months I drive, I will not have the car stereo on. After the first two months, after clearing this with my parents, I will be allowed to have the stereo on but will make no adjustments to it other than changing the volume while driving. Under no circumstances will I change a CD while driving. I will change these only when stopped or pulled over.

5. *Other electronics.* I will not use cell phones, MP3 players, or any other electronic device while driving. I will pull over for operation of cell phones and electronic equipment.

6. *No rushing.* Accidents are more likely to happen when I rush. I am more likely to rush when I leave late. Therefore, my parents reserve the right not to allow me to drive unless I leave by a time they specify. For example, if my parents tell me that I must allow twenty minutes to get to something that starts at 7:00, I may not leave later than 6:40. In such cases when leaving later than the specified time, my parents will attempt to provide alternative transportation, to whatever extent possible.

7. *Attention to driving.* I will not do things while driving that distract me from the road. No applying makeup, getting things in and out of a purse or backpack, and so on.

SPECIAL ITEMS

1. *Tickets and moving violations* will result in suspension of my driving privileges for a period to be determined by my parents.

My parents have no obligation to pay my fines for driving-related tickets.

2. *Financial.* I will make certain financial contributions to the purchase of the car, maintenance of the car, and/or insurance. My contributions are currently as follows: _____

_____.

3. *Family obligations.* I agree to provide transportation to family members at the directive of my parents. Fulfilling these obligations is a condition of my use of a car. Sometimes these responsibilities will override my own desires and interests in using the car.

4. *General life responsibilities.* I agree that I must be responsible to drive safely and that my parents must believe I am relatively responsible in order to allow me to drive. They may, therefore, take into account how I handle my general responsibilities, including schoolwork, employment, household duties. I will also maintain a respectful attitude. I will not ask my parents to allow me to drive when I am rude and disrespectful to them or to others.

5. *Right to clear expectations.* My parents have a right to expect me to be responsible. I have a right to be told what this means. For this reason, I may ask my parents for clarification of their requirement that I "be responsible."

6. *Changes in this agreement.* I understand that this contract will be made stricter at any time my parents believe that is the best thing to do. I understand that if I consistently abide by these rules that my parents will work with me to make the contract less strict as I gain experience. However, I understand that, bottom line, it is my parents' choice and responsibility to change or not change the contract. We will review this agreement and

perhaps make changes to it on _____ (date)
or earlier if my parents or I wish to do so.

SUMMARY

I agree to abide by the rules in this contract, and I accept the consequences and penalties if I do not. I recognize my parents' authority in deciding if I may drive. That authority is final until I am an adult living independent of my parents.

Signatures

DRIVER _____   _____ (date)
PARENT(s)/Guardian(s)

_____   _____ (date)
_____   _____ (date)

NOTES TO PARENTS
ON THE DRIVING CONTRACT

1. Remember that this contract covers the first days or weeks that the young driver is driving. Keep that in mind when considering how strict to be. You should plan to revise the contract after a month or so.

2. Rule 1 in Category A, regarding alcohol and drug use. Some parents read this as a kind of acknowledgment that their child will drink alcohol or do drugs. This is a fair objection, but it is also true that many teens drink and do drugs. Research data released in 2005 indicate that 21 percent of young people between the ages of sixteen and twenty admit to drinking and/

or using drugs *and driving under the influence*. Because this is so critical, I believe it is important to address it in the contract. You may want to consider changing the rule to allow you to suspend driving privileges if your young person drinks or does drugs at all. Or if you keep the rule something like it is in this contract, you can tell your teenager that you do not approve of drinking or drugs at any time.

3. Rule 2, Category B, Curfew. Some parents believe this is overly strict and unrealistic. I added this to the contract after research established that a 10:00 P.M. to 5:00 P.M. curfew on driving reduces the risk of accidents. You may, of course, alter this requirement if you feel it is unrealistic in your child's situation. However, remember that this contract is intended to be reviewed and revised regularly. In its present form, it is intended to cover the first weeks of driving.

4. Parents often correctly point out that some of these rules can be broken without your knowledge. I agree. In spite of this, I believe it is important to include the rules anyway. You *may* discover violations and, in any case, you have communicated to your teenager a rule you intend they follow. Be hopeful that, if not eliminating the behavior, it may at least reduce it.

5. Rule 3, Category B, Limit on Passengers. This is an essential rule. There is a very direct relationship between the number of passengers in the car with a teenage driver and the likelihood of an accident. It also, of course, increases the number of potential deaths or injuries. We highly recommend not exceeding a limit of one passenger during the first year of driving.

6. Rules 9 and 10, Category C, Cell phones, Car stereos, and other electronics. Consider starting with a strict policy: no stereo at all

during the first weeks of driving. In a later revision of the contract, consider a rule that they may have the stereo on, but they may not manipulate any controls while in motion. *We believe the use of cell phones and MP3 players, iPods, and the like while driving is particularly dangerous.*

7. "Getting it." Recently, I've been thinking about a concern I have about contracts of this type: teenagers may quickly sign it, without really "learning" the rules. Even if they do learn them, they may forget them. So I encourage you to think of creative ways to assure that they have really understood and retained the rules. Here are a few suggestions:
    a. Require your child to read the entire contract to you, aloud.
    b. Require your child to sit while you read it to them.
    c. Before signing, sit down together, read each item together, and discuss.
    d. Occasionally ask questions, such as, "What does the contract say about curfew?"

8. Negotiating. Consider this approach: make a draft of the contract before you present it to your child, and be sure to include some items you are willing to adjust, negotiate, or even give up. Instead of giving the child a finished contract, offer to go through it with him or her item by item and invite the teenager to make a "counter-proposal." It's perfectly all right to make some rules non-negotiable.[1]

Notes

Individual stories designated throughout with initials and states are used with the permission of those authors. Names are omitted to preserve privacy.

INTRODUCTION

1. Sherrell Willis, as quoted in the *New Haven Independent* (New Haven, CT).

CHAPTER 1: P–T–E: PLEASE, THANK YOU, AND EXCUSE ME

1. As seen in *Dear Abby* by Abigail Van Buren a.k.a. Jeanne Phillips and founded by her mother Pauline Phillips. ©2007 Universal Press Syndicate. Reprinted with permission. All rights reserved.

CHAPTER 2: SPANKING, TIME-OUTS, AND OTHER EIGHT-LETTER WORDS

1. Thomas Szasz, *The Second Sin* (Doubleday: New York 1973).
2. American Academy of Pediatrics, "*AAP* Survey on Corporal Punishment Reveals Divergent Views," Periodic Survey of Fellows, No. 38, from the Division of Child Health Research, www.aap.org/research/periodicsurvey/ps38a.htm.
3. Michelle O'Neil, as quoted on www.imperfectparent.com. Used by permission.

4. American Academy of Child and Adolescent Psychiatry, "Child Abuse—
    The Hidden Bruises," Facts for Families, No. 5; updated July 2004, www.
    aacap.org/cs/root/facts_for_families/child_abuse_the_hidden_bruises.

5. Katherine J. Aucoin, Paul J. Frick, S. Doug Bodin, "Corporal
    Punishment and Child Adjustment," *Journal of Applied Developmental
    Psychology*, Volume 27, Issue 6, Nov–Dec 2006.

CHAPTER 4: FAIR OR FOUL: SPORTSMANSHIP

1. Michael Josephson, "What Are Your Children Learning? The Impact of
    High School Sports on the Values and Ethics of High School Athletes"
    (report by the Josephson Institute of Ethics, Los Angeles, CA 2006).

2. Ibid.

3. Ibid.

CHAPTER 5: THE DRESS CODE

1. While fighting in the Pacific during World War II, General Douglas
    MacArthur—whose father was Civil War hero Lieutenant-General
    Arthur MacArthur—wrote a letter to his son, Arthur IV, which contains
    this quote.

CHAPTER 6: TEENAGERS: THE ALIEN YEARS

1. Linda Patia Spear, PhD, "Neurodevelopment During Adolescence,"
    Neurodevelopmental Mechanisms in Psychopathology, Cambridge
    University Press, Nov. 2003.

2. Nanci Hellmich, "Parents Want to Be Teens' Pals," *USA Today*, 12
    October 2004.

3. Shel Franco, "Behavior Contracts: What Can They Do for You? An
    interview with Mark Kichler, President of KidsContracts, Inc.,"
    www.teenagerstoday.com/articles/teenagers/behavior-contracts-1078.

4. Sean McDowell, "Straight Talk on Sex." Used by permission.

CHAPTER 7: DRIVING, DATING, AND OTHER DEATH-DEFYING FEATS

1. Insurance Institute for Highway Safety, "Fatality Facts 2006: Teenagers,"
    www.iihs.org/research/fatality_facts_2006/teenagers.html.

2. Ibid.

3. Ibid.
4. Kenneth Adams, "The Effectiveness of Juvenile Curfews at Crime Prevention," *The Annals of the American Academy of Political and Social Science*, Volume 587 (2003): 136–59.

CHAPTER 8: THE NOT-SO-GOOD, THE PRETTY BAD, AND THE REALLY UGLY

1. NIDA InfoFacts: Inhalants, www.nida.nih.gov/Infofacts/Inhalants. html; the National Institute on Drug Abuse (NIDA) is part of the National Institutes of Health (NIH), a component of the United States Department of Health and Human Services, Washington, DC.
2. Eric H. Chudler, http://faculty.washington.edu/chudler/coca.html. Used by permission.
3. "Partnership Unveils Time to Talk, A New Cause-Related Marketing Campaign," 25 April 2007. © Partnership for a Drug-Free America, www.theantidrug.com/advice/advice_start_convo.asp.
4. Debbie Kellogg, www.timetotalk.org. Used by permission.
5. Drug Facts: Cocaine, Office of National Drug Control Policy, www.whitehousedrugpolicy.gov/drugfact/cocaine/index.html.
6. "What America's Users Spend on Illegal Drugs 1988–2000," Office of National Drug Control Policy, www.whitehousedrugpolicy.gov/publications/pdf/american_users_spend_2002.pdf.
7. "Attorney General Lawrence Wasden Brings Girl Talk: Choices and Consequences of Underage Drinking to Fort Boise High School to Address Alarming Data on Moms, Daughters, and Underage Drinking," The Century Council, 13 March 2008, www.centurycouncil.org/press/2008/pr2008-03-13b.html.
8. Town of Barnstable, Regulatory Services Department, 7–8, 15 December 2003, www.town.barnstable.ma.us/ConsumerAffairs/LicensingAuthority/Minutes/121503MinutesHearing.pdf.
9. "Teen Drinking Shocker," 4 Jan. 2003, CBS News, http://www.cbsnews.com/stories/2003/01/04/eveningnews/main535289.shtml.
10. Robert A. Clifford, "Parents Can Be Liable for Their Kids' Drinking," *Clifford's Notes*, Chicago Lawyer, 1 September 2007, www.cliffordlaw.com/news/attorneys-articles/parents-can-be-liable-for-their-kids2019-drinking.

11. "Attorney General Lawrence Wasden Brings Girl Talk: Choices and Consequences of Underage Drinking to Fort Boise High School to Address Alarming Data on Moms, Daughters, and Underage Drinking," The Century Council, 13 March 2008, www.centurycouncil.org/press/2008/pr2008-03-13b.html.

12. Vanessa O'Connell, "Underage Drinking at Home," *The Wall Street Journal*, 15 Sept. 2004, azcentral.com, www.azcentral.com/families/articles/0915fam_teendrinking.html.

13. Underage Drinking Facts, North Carolina Department of Crime Control and Public Safety, www.nccrimecontrol.org/Index2.cfm?a=000003,000005,000272,000273.

14. "Underage Drinking: A Growing Health Care Concern," National Institute on Alcohol Abuse and Alcoholism, National Institutes of Health, Department of Health and Human Services, http://pubs.niaaa.nih.gov/publications/PSA/underagepg2.htm.

15. John E. Donovan, "Children Are Introduced to Sipping and Tasting Alcohol in the Home," *Alcoholism: Clinical & Experimental Research* (January 6, 2008).

16. Insurance Institute for Highway Safety, "Fatality Facts 2006: Teenagers," www.iihs.org/research/fatality_facts_2006/teenagers.html. Used by permission.

17. "Underage Drinking—Not a Harmless Rite of Passage," 19 April 2004, Hazelden, www.hazelden.org/web/public/prev40419.page.

18. State Profiles of Underage Drinking Laws, Alcohol Policy Information System, National Institute on Alcohol Abuse and Alcoholism, National Institutes of Health, Department of Health and Human Services, www.alcoholpolicy.niaaa.nih.gov/stateprofiles.

19. Abbie Vansickle, "Did Parent Let Teens Drink, Drive?" *St. Petersburg Times*, 11 July 2007, www.sptimes.com/2007/07/11/Hillsborough/Did_parent_let_teens_.shtml.

20. Emma Schwartz, "A Host of Trouble," *U.S. News and World Report*, 29 September 2007, www.usnews.com/articles/news/national/2007/09/29/more-parents-are-being-held-criminally-liable-for-teens-drinking-parties.html.

21. "Teen Drinking Shocker—Underage Drinking Troublespot," 3 January 2004, Teenagers Against Alcohol Abuse, www.ta3info.org/news030104.html.

22. Daniela Deane, "Justice is Unequal for Parents Who Host Teen Drinking Parties," *Washington Post*, 4 July 2007, www.compelledtoact.com/Involvement_pages/State/Justice_Unequal.htm.

23. "Are You Doing Your Part?" The Century Council, www.centurycouncil.org/underage/65_percent.html.

24. National Survey on Drug Use and Health: National Findings, Office of National Drug Control Policy, www.whitehousedrugpolicy.gov/NEWS/press05/090805fs.html.

25. Underage Drinking Fact Sheet, The Century Council, www.centurycouncil.org/underage/65_data.html.

26. Underage Drinking Facts, North Carolina Department of Crime Control and Public Safety, www.nccrimecontrol.org/Index2.cfm?a=000003,000005,000272,000273.

Appendix B: Sample of Driving Contract
1. Dale Wisely, www.parentingteendrivers.com. Used by permission.

About the Author

E. D. Hill joined Fox News Channel (FNC) in March of 1998. Hill is a Fox News host and a regular fill-in on the number one ranked *The O'Reilly Factor* weeknights on FNC. She was also coanchor for *Fox & Friends*, the network's weekday morning program, and from 2002 to 2007, she was cohost with Bill O'Reilly on his radio program *The O'Reilly Factor*. Prior to joining FNC, Hill was a contributing reporter for ABC News' *Good Morning America*, covering family issues.

During her broadcasting career, Hill has served as anchor for the ABC flagship station in New York, WABC-TV, and for WHDH-TV (NBC in Boston) where she won a local Emmy Award for Outstanding News Special. Earlier in her career, Hill was a business anchor for CBS Morning News and CBS Radio Network and the anchor for WPXI-TV's (NBC in Pittsburgh) evening newscasts.

A graduate of the University of Texas and the mother of eight children, Hill is also the recipient of a Golden Quill Award for live spot news reporting.